W9-CCB-922

HUNTINGTON LIBRARY PUBLICATIONS

ROWLANDSON'S DRAWINGS FOR *THE ENGLISH DANCE OF DEATH*

ROWLANDSON'S DRAWINGS FOR *THE ENGLISH DANCE OF DEATH*

WITH AN INTRODUCTION AND NOTES BY ROBERT R. WARK

THE HUNTINGTON LIBRARY, SAN MARINO, CALIFORNIA

1966

LIBRARY OF CONGRESS CATALOG CARD NUMBER 66-21941
PRINTED BY ANDERSON, RITCHIE & SIMON
DESIGNED BY WARD RITCHIE

PREFACE

ALTHOUGH THIS VOLUME forms a self-contained study, it was also conceived as a companion to *Rowlandson's Drawings for a Tour in a Post Chaise*, published by the Huntington Library in 1963. The two series of drawings stand close to the terminal points of Rowlandson's career, and they exemplify complementary phases of his personality.

About half the known drawings connected with *The English Dance of Death* are in the Huntington Library; the rest are scattered through various public and private collections. I wish to express my thanks to the owners and custodians of these drawings for their courtesy during the course of this study. It is particularly pleasant to recall the generous and cooperative spirit in which the many requests for information and assistance were received.

I owe a special debt of gratitude to the Visitors of the Ashmolean Museum for their extraordinary kindness in permitting the four Dance of Death drawings in their charge to be sent to the Huntington Library for direct comparison with related material.

Mr. John Hayes, of the London Museum, read the text in manuscript and made many helpful suggestions. Mr. Luke Herrmann, of the Ashmolean Museum, has given me the benefit of his knowledge of Rowlandson and has endured with great patience innumerable inquiries in connection with the four Ashmolean drawings.

I am grateful to the following individuals and institutions for permission to reproduce drawings in their possession: Mr. Philip Hofer, Mr. Paul Mellon, Dr. Morris Saffron, the Art Museum at Princeton University, the Ashmolean Museum, the Harry Elkins Widener Collection in the Harvard College Library, the Henry E. Huntington Library and Art Gallery, the Spencer Collection in the New York Public Library.

The publication of this book was made possible through the generosity of the trustees of the Huntington Library and the Friends of the Huntington Library.

ROBERT R. WARK

San Marino, California
May 1965

CONTENTS

SOME DATES IN THE LIFE OF THOMAS ROWLANDSON

1757 (or 1756) Thomas Rowlandson born on July 14 in the Old Jewry, London, son of a textile merchant, William Rowlandson.

1759 William Rowlandson declared bankrupt. Thomas placed in the care of his uncle and aunt, James and Jane Rowlandson.

1764 Death of James Rowlandson. Thomas left henceforth in the care of his aunt.

1772 Entered the Royal Academy Schools on November 6.

Mid-1770's Visited Paris for an undetermined length of time.

1775 First exhibited at the Royal Academy.

1784 Exhibited "Vauxhall" and "The Serpentine River"; September-October, probable time of the "Tour in a Post Chaise."

1786 Exhibited "An English Review" and "A French Review."

1787 Last exhibited at the Royal Academy.

1789 Death of Rowlandson's aunt, by whose will Rowlandson received approximately £2,000.

1789 Traveled with Henry Wigstead to Brighthelmstone (Brighton). Published a series of prints commemorating the trip, with text by Wigstead, in 1790.

1797 Traveled with Wigstead in north and south Wales. A book commemorating the journey was published in 1800.

Late 1790's Began association with the publisher Rudolph Ackermann, for whom Rowlandson executed a great quantity of graphic work throughout the remainder of his career. Also met one of his most consistent patrons, the banker Matthew Michell.

1800 Death of Wigstead.

1808-1811 *The Microcosm of London*, 3 vols., with colored plates by Rowlandson and Augustus Charles Pugin, published by Ackermann.

1812-1821 The three *Dr. Syntax* tours, with illustrations by Rowlandson and text by W. Combe, published by Ackermann.

1814-1816 Rowlandson working on designs for *The English Dance of Death.*

1827 Died on April 21. Buried in St. Paul's, Covent Garden.

INTRODUCTION

I

THE DANCE OF DEATH found a sympathetic interpreter in Thomas Rowlandson. His art frequently involves a combination of apparent opposites: themes in which the sinister and even repulsive are given a prominent place but are treated with grotesque humor in an artistic vocabulary of great elegance and decorative appeal. Given such inclinations, it would have been almost surprising if during the course of his long and prolific career Rowlandson had not attempted a Dance of Death. His treatment of it constitutes one of the most extended and sustained products of his peculiar brand of imaginative and artistic genius.

When Rowlandson produced the drawings for *The English Dance of Death* (mostly between 1814 and 1816), he was an artist of established reputation with the major portion of his career behind him. After some lean years around the turn of the century he had become reasonably popular and prosperous. He was in his late fifties. There was still a busy decade of activity ahead, with hundreds of designs yet to come from his restless pen. But none of these rival *The English Dance of Death* for the consistently high level of invention and execution maintained in the elaboration of a single theme. It is his last major work.

The English Dance of Death, as it was presented to the public, was a cooperative venture. Certainly Rowlandson's designs are the essential and immeasurably the most important part of the publication. But it is doubtful if he ever would have executed the drawings without the interest and encouragement of Rudolph Ackermann and the cooperation of William Combe. Combe produced two volumes of verses, which (although rather dismal in themselves) were thought to enhance the designs for the general public. Ackermann was the promoter and publisher, who doubtless supplied the initiative for the project in the first place and certainly was the sole financial backer. The three had combined forces previously, notably in the third volume of *The Microcosm of London* (1811) and *The Tour of Doctor Syntax in Search of the Picturesque* (1812). They were later to produce *The Dance of Life* (1817) and two further tours of Dr. Syntax in 1820 and 1821.

On the surface, at least, the men do not appear a particularly compatible trio. Rowlandson and Combe were temperamentally so different that it is improbable they ever had much to do with one another. Combe was some sixteen years older than Rowlandson, having been born in Bristol in 1741. He was brought up in the pattern of a fashionable gentleman, going to Eton and Oxford, and rounding out his education with an extended grand tour in France and Italy. When he returned to England, he "lived in a most princely style, and, though a bachelor, kept two carriages, several horses, and a large retinue of servants. . . . He was generally recognised by the appellation of 'Count Coombe'" (*Bristol Observer*, July 16, 1823). But his fortune (according to the author of the obituary notice in the *Gentleman's Magazine*, August 1823) "he soon dissipated among the high connections to which his talents and attainments introduced him, and he subsequently passed through many vicissitudes of life, which at length compelled him to resort to Literature for support. . . . A love of show and dress, but neither gaming or drinking, was the source of his embarrassments. He was indeed remarkably abstemious, drinking nothing but water till the last few weeks of his life, when wine was recommended to him as a medicine."

There are, to be sure, some parallels between this chronicle and Rowlandson's biography. Rowlandson never went to Eton or Oxford, but he did have an indulgent aunt who provided a good education for her nephew, supported him for travel and study in France, and eventually left him a comfortable bequest. Like Combe, Rowlandson seems to have dissipated his inheritance; at least he was reduced to meager financial circumstances during the last few years of the century. Rowlandson, however, was anything but a teetotaler. Though the anecdotes concerning his gambling and general carousing are probably exaggerated, there can be little doubt that these pastimes were principal sources of recreation and that Rowlandson could have had little patience with Combe's abstemious yet ostentatious tendencies.

Both men appear to owe their financial recovery primarily to their association with the publisher Rudolph Ackermann. Rowlandson and Combe were almost incredibly prolific, and most of Rowlandson's output after 1800, and Combe's after 1810, was placed with Ackermann. The article on Combe in the *Dictionary of National Biography* credits him with eighty-six books, and this does not include a great quantity of more ephemeral writing and editing for which he was responsible. Rowlandson's industry as a draftsman must have almost equaled Combe's as a writer.

Combe is now remembered primarily because of his connection with the Dr. Syntax volumes, and these in turn retain their interest because of Rowlandson's designs. For some reason (which one must confess is not entirely apparent from either the designs or the text) the initial *Tour of Doctor Syntax in Search of the Picturesque* was immensely successful, running through five editions between its first appearance in 1812 and the end of 1813. Doubtless it was the success of this venture that prompted Ackermann to promote the publication of *The English Dance of Death* beginning in April of 1814.

Ackermann must have been an unusually enterprising, energetic, and generally attractive person. He was born in Stolberg, Saxony, in 1764, the son of a coach-builder and harness maker. His interests developed in the direction of designing rather than building coaches. After studying this craft in Paris, he settled in London, apparently sometime in the 1780's. For about ten years he continued to design coaches, and he was responsible for such important models as the coach built for the lord lieutenant of Ireland in 1790 and one for the lord mayor of Dublin in 1791. As late as 1805 he was entrusted with the preparation of Lord Nelson's funeral car, and even in 1818-1820 he was occupied with a patent for a movable axle for carriages.

But after 1795 Ackermann's primary interests shifted, and in that year he opened a print shop in the Strand. Henceforth his major professional concern was as a fine-art publisher and bookseller. In this connection he was largely responsible for the development of lithography as an independent print process in England. Rowlandson's association with Ackermann must have begun shortly after the shop was opened. Joseph Grego records four Rowlandson prints published by Ackermann in 1797, and the volume increases thereafter very quickly.

Ackermann was of a particularly humanitarian turn of mind, and he devoted a great deal of time and energy to helping refugees and others who suffered during the French Revolution and Napoleonic wars. An informative essay on Ackermann in *Notes and Queries* (4th Ser., Vol. IV [1869]) records that "During the period in which French emigrants were numerous in this country, Mr. Ackermann was one of the first to find a liberal employment for them. He had seldom less than fifty nobles, priests, and ladies engaged upon screens, card-racks, flower-stands and other ornamental work. This manufacture was so well-established in favour that after 1802, when the emigrants could return to France, it furnished employment for a great number of our compatriots" (p. 110).

Ackermann was also a chief supporter of the relief measures undertaken to alleviate the misery in Germany, particularly Saxony, following the Battle of Leipzig in 1813. "With the help of the Duke of Sussex he got a committee together in Westminster and in the city of London: the first obtained a parliamentary grant of 100,000 *l.*, and the second furnished a rather larger sum in private contributions. . . . For two years Mr. Ackermann undertook the task of correspondence with the German committee for distributing those sums, of examination into the urgency of each appeal for help, and of dividing the fund" (*N&Q*, p. 111).

Once again, following the influx of Spanish refugees after 1815, Ackermann proved a great source of support: "He not only spent large sums in procuring Spanish translations of English works and original Spanish elementary books, and in publishing them, but established branch book and print shops in many of the chief towns across the Atlantic. The value of this contribution to the advancement of Southern America was acknowledged by President Bolivar in a letter dated at Bogota, December 15, 1827" (*N&Q*, p. 111).

These, then, were the three men jointly responsible for *The English Dance of Death*—a highly interesting but oddly assorted group. Throughout their joint productions Rowlandson and Combe seem to have preserved a Gilbert-and-Sullivan type of relationship, with Ackermann acting as the intermediary. Combe himself, in the Advertisement to the first volume of *The English Dance of Death*, outlined the procedure followed: "His [Rowlandson's] Pencil has accordingly produced the Designs, which, in the Order they were delivered to me, I have accompanied with Metrical Illustrations: a Mode of proceeding which has been sanctioned by the Success of our joint Labours in the 'Tour of Doctor Syntax.'" And in the preface to *The Tour of Doctor Syntax in Search of the Picturesque* (1812) Combe has given a somewhat more detailed account of the working relationship with Rowlandson for that project: "An Etching or a Drawing was accordingly sent to me every month, and I composed a certain proportion of pages in verse, in which, of course, the subject of the design was included: the rest depended upon what my imagination could furnish.—When the first print was sent to me, I did not know what would be the subject of the second; and in this manner, in a great measure, the Artist continued designing, and I continued writing, every month for two years, 'till a work, containing near ten thousand Lines was produced: the Artist and the Writer having no personal communication with, or knowledge of each other."

There is one drawing in the Dance of Death series that sheds a little more light on the working relationship between Combe and Rowlandson. It is the sketch for "Tom Higgins," the fifth subject in the series, and it has the following penciled inscription on the back in Combe's handwriting: "man asleep could [illegible] change [illegible] red cap for a wig & his slippers for shoes, it would suit me better. If he were a little better dressed and more as if he were an Esquire I should be glad." The suggested changes, the wig for the cap, and shoes for the slippers, were certainly adopted in the print. It would thus seem that at least in this instance Combe had some small influence on the finished design. The fact that such a comment should be written out at all lends weight to Combe's statement that the designs passed from Rowlandson to himself without the two men meeting. The issue is of importance when considering the extent to which Combe's text may be relied upon as a commentary on Rowlandson's drawings. The little evidence at hand is not encouraging. Simply on the face of it, the connection between the plates and Combe's text is often merely tangential. A further discrepancy frequently exists between the two lines of verse beneath each print and the rest of the text. The two lines sometimes appear hand-printed and written on small scraps of paper associated with the actual drawings. They were probably, although not unquestionably, written by Rowlandson himself. In any event, they are close to him and would appear to reflect more accurately than Combe's text what the artist wished us to read in the drawing. This being the case, there seemed little reason for more than quadrupling the size of this book by including Combe's verses.

The prints as they were published follow Rowlandson's drawings very closely. Only in one or two instances is there even a minor departure from the preliminary design. There is no reason to suppose that the prints were actually executed by Rowlandson. The title page reads "from the designs of Thomas Rowlandson," a wording that would hardly have been adopted if the artist himself had etched the plates.

The plates were first executed in line etching. A number of proofs must have been pulled at this stage. There is a complete set of these in the Huntington Library, and several individual impressions with watercolor added are known elsewhere. The plates were next enriched with aquatint washes. Judging from the four copies of the book at the Huntington Library, these washes were renewed and strengthened, probably at the time the separate numbers were gathered together and issued as two volumes. Some indications concerning these various "states" have been given in the notes on the individual subjects. Finally, the impressions were colored by hand. It is clear once again from the copies available that a color scheme was adopted for each plate, the colors then being applied in an assembly-line fashion by the workers in Ackermann's shop. There is no apparent connection between the colors used on the plates and those in the original drawings.

The book appeared in serial form, three prints being issued each month, with accompanying text, from April 1, 1814, until March 1, 1816. There were thus twenty-four numbers in all. Contrary to the impression created by some students, the numbers did not form part of Ackermann's magazine, *Repository of Arts*, but were issued independently from Ackermann's shop.

The bibliographical history of the publication is not clear in all details. Direct comparative examination of the four copies in the Huntington Library reveals many minor variations in both text and plates that suggest various stages in the preparation of the book. A title page was apparently printed up when the series began, and reads: *English Dance of Death, / in / Twenty-four Monthly Numbers, / from the Designs of / Thomas Rowlandson / accompanied with / Metrical Illustrations, / by the Author of / "Doctor Syntax." / Vol. 1. / London: / Printed by J. Diggens, St. Ann's Lane; / Published at R. Ackermann's Repository of Arts, 101, Strand; / and to be had of / all the Book and Print-sellers in the United Kingdom / 1814.* The one really interesting piece of information disclosed by this page is that the length of the series had evidently been determined from the outset.

A second title page appears to have been printed when Volume I was complete in 1815. It differs considerably from the first: *The / English Dance of Death, / from the Designs of / Thomas Rowlandson, / with / Metrical Illustrations, / by the Author of / "Doctor Syntax." / Pallida Mors aquo pulsat pede pauperum tabernas / Regumque turres. Hor. Lib. I. Od. 4. / — With equal Pace, impartial Fate / Knocks at the Palace, as the Cottage Gate. / Vol. I. / London: / Printed by J. Diggens, St. Ann's Lane; / Published at R. Ackermann's Repository of Arts, 101, Strand; / and to be had of / All the Book and Print-sellers in the United Kingdom. / 1815.*

Another title page was added for the second volume in 1816. This is identical with the preceding except for the date and volume number. Finally an engraved title page was supplied in front of the printed one for the first volume, and this engraving bears the date March 1, 1816, the day on which the last three prints in the series were issued.

The book seems to have been only moderately successful. Aside from the internal evidence offered by alterations in the plates and the text, there is no indication of any sequence of editions. It never attained the popularity of the Dr. Syntax tours, although in *The English Dance of Death* both artist and writer were working on a distinctly higher level. It stands as the most impressive achievement of the Rowlandson-Combe-Ackermann trio.

II

The theme of the Dance of Death has a long history stretching back centuries before Rowlandson's involvement with it. The subject has had a curious attraction for artists, writers, and scholars, and there is a vast literature dealing with the topic. It would be pretentious to rehearse all this data in detail, partly because it is readily available elsewhere but also because Rowlandson's connection with the tradition is not particularly close. Nevertheless, Rowlandson's achievement cannot be properly assessed without some knowledge of the earlier treatments of the theme.

The Dance of Death, in the narrow and strict sense of the term, is an art form that emerged in late medieval times, although its ultimate sources and origins are lost in antiquity. Normally the pictorial side of the work consists of a series of human figures each accompanied by a skeleton or cadaver that came to symbolize Death. The figure of Death is frequently represented as if in a grotesque dance to which he is leading his human companion. The human figures are drawn from the various strata of society in more or less descending order: Pope, Emperor, Cardinal, King, Bishop, Duke, and so on, down to the Parish Priest and the Laborer. The order and number of figures vary a great deal from one rendition to another, but the general theme of Death leading away members of the various ranks of society remains the same. The pictures usually are accompanied by a text which takes the form of a series of brief conversations between the human figures and Death. The meaning behind the presentation is clear enough: Death visits all ranks and conditions of men; he is the great leveler before whom all worldly distinctions crumble. The sentiment is much the same as that embodied in the quotation from Horace included on the title page of *The English Dance of Death*: "Pallida Mors æquo pulsat pede pauperum tabernas, Regumque turres."

There is much dispute among scholars concerning precisely where and when the Dance of Death first appeared in the developed form in which it became so widely known. The representation that is usually given priority was executed in 1424-1425 in the Cemetery of the Innocents, Paris. The theme was very popular during the remaining years of the fifteenth century, and presentations of it from this period exist or are known to have existed in many parts of Europe. Very often these took the form of wall decorations in churches and cemeteries, but by the late fifteenth century the subject was also appearing frequently in printed books.

The culmination of this activity, at least from the artistic point of view, came in 1538 with the publication in Lyons of Hans Holbein's great Dance of Death. Holbein had been concerned with the theme for many years. In the 1520's he produced a series of designs for a small Dance of Death in which the subject is interwoven with an alphabet, and it was probably at about this same time that he began working on the forty-nine designs for the larger work. Both sets were transcribed into woodcuts by Hans Lützelburger, a gifted craftsman who certainly must be credited with a large share of the success of the publications.

Holbein in the 1538 publication follows the generally established pattern for the subject but with some significant modifications. In each instance the meeting between Death and the human figure is developed into a scene, and thus the narrative and dramatic possibilities of the theme are greatly enlarged. Holbein's concern, however, remains clearly with the basic idea of Death encountering representatives of the various levels of society.

The vast majority of the subsequent treatments of the Dance of Death derive from, or at least are strongly influenced by, Holbein's work. The designs were reissued almost unchanged at least fifty times before the end of the eighteenth century, and they served as the point of departure for most of the other interpretations of the subject. Holbein's Dance of Death thus becomes the standard gauge against which all subsequent treatments of the theme are measured.

Rowlandson's production, viewed in this context, is a distinctly unusual affair. In the first place, the designs are not concerned with treating the various levels of society. Rowlandson discards the pattern on which the normal Dance of Death was constructed. Although the quotation from Horace on the title page suggests that the theme is the universality and the leveling character of Death, Rowlandson is in fact little concerned with this traditional aspect of the subject. His interest lies more with the situation in which Death appears than with the idea that Death is inevitable for all conditions of men. Thus the whole meaning of the art form is changed. The didactic and moralizing note of the normal Dance of Death largely evaporates. It must be admitted that in dropping this aspect of his subject Rowlandson loses the basic unifying theme that usually gives coherence to the work. Nor has he supplied any adequate substitute. His Dance of Death is in essence a series of incidents, not connected in any pattern or design except the continual appearance of Death. The force of the series rests on the variety of incidents the artist is able to present and the ingenuity with which he treats them.

The change in emphasis is entirely in accord with Rowlandson's personality. He is neither a moralist nor a satirist. The opportunities which the theme offers in these directions have little appeal for him. He is primarily an observer and reporter who presents us with a very detailed view of the society in which he moves. He is constantly emphasizing the humorous side of what he sees, but generally with no discernible didactic intention. His Dance of Death is not a parody or caricature of the theme. But a spirit akin to the humorous exaggeration of caricature is often apparent. Occasionally a sense of indignation may lie behind the humor; and this is more frequently the case with the Dance of Death designs than with most of his subjects. It seems, for instance, that he is distinctly out of sympathy with the medical profession. Generally, however, he has no axe to grind.

The most obvious weakness in Rowlandson's presentation of the Dance of Death is probably his uncertain vacillation between humor and pathos. Many of the designs are surely intended to be funny; many others just as surely are not. But Rowlandson's style and artistic vocabulary are not readily adaptable to the serious and pathetic. His innate tendency to caricature, his ebullient line, and his decorative color consistently combine to create a gay and good-humored effect regardless of the subject. Unlike his great contemporary Goya, Rowlandson is not in control of the means to evoke a wide range of emotional reactions, even if he may wish to do so.

The path Rowlandson takes, away from the emphasis on Death encountering all ranks of society toward a more narrative and anecdotal emphasis on the situations in which Death may occur, is not entirely new. Holbein himself had moved the Dance of Death strongly in that direction by developing each encounter as a scene with supporting characters and incidents. It is significant in this respect that the title actually given to the Holbein series by the publisher was not Dance of Death at all, but *Les simulachres & historiees faces de la mort* (the images and storied aspects of death).

Several post-Holbein treatments of the subject depart much farther from the early form of the Dance, and some of these (especially in the eighteenth century) begin to approach Rowlandson's point of view. One of the more interesting appeared in Nuremberg in 1736: *Schau-Platz des Todes, oder Todten-Tanz*, by Salomon Van Rusting. This includes, besides several of the traditional subjects, Death at a masquerade and Death with a group of skaters, both subjects used by Rowlandson. Another series, *Freund Heins Erscheinungen in Holbeins Manier*, by J. R. Schellenberg, appeared in Winterthur in 1785. It also includes several subjects in which the emphasis is on the incident rather than on the social position of the person meeting Death. Some of these, such as the suicide, Death visiting a lady at her toilet, the schoolmaster, the lottery, and the recruiting officer, are subjects that also appear among Rowlandson's designs.

Curiously enough these German treatments of the theme are at least as close in spirit to Rowlandson as any that actually appeared in England during the eighteenth century. It is possible that Ackermann, who probably knew the German works, brought them to

Rowlandson's attention. But certainly the similarities are not sufficiently close to insist upon such a connection.

At least one English version of the Dance of Death, produced by Richard Newton in 1796, has some resemblance to Rowlandson's. The prints themselves are apparently rare; there is no copy in the British Museum. But Francis Douce supplied a detailed description in the introduction to his edition of Holbein's Dance of Death in 1833. Newton's Dance contains only twenty-eight subjects, against Rowlandson's seventy-two, but there is an apparent interest in situations as well as social types, and an air of caricature pervades the work. There are several subjects similar to those treated by Rowlandson: the gamblers; the scolding wife; the undertaker; the physician, gravedigger, and Death dancing a round; the doctor, sick patient, and nurse; the watchman; the barber; the lady and Death reflected in the mirror; the amorous old man and young woman; the miser; the female gin drinker.

G. M. Woodward's *Dance of Death Modernised*, which appeared in 1800, is more of a genuine parody of the traditional presentation than is the work of either Newton or Rowlandson. Woodward returns to various social types for his subjects, and it is only the element of caricature that has any relation to Rowlandson's handling of the subject.

Considering the strength of the Dance of Death tradition, and the great number of treatments of it that would have been readily available to Rowlandson, his independence and originality are all the more noticeable. Indeed, it is difficult to escape the conclusion that if he was not actually ignorant of the rich artistic background of the theme with which he was dealing, he must have been at least generally indifferent to it. Even in those instances when he treats a subject handled by a predecessor there seems to be no evidence of any visual recollection of the earlier design. His own imagination is clearly the primary source from which he draws inspiration. When he does borrow, it is likely to be from one of his own earlier drawings rather than from another artist.

The Dance of Death continued to fascinate the public long after Rowlandson's treatment of the theme had ceased to be generally available. Holbein's designs remained the most popular and were the source to which most artists looked for guidance. There were a few later volumes that followed the semihumorous attitude of Rowlandson (*The British Dance of Death* [ca. 1825]; *Death's Doings* [1826]; *Death's Ramble* [1827]). But clearly the Victorian period would find levity in the treatment of such a subject distasteful. It was not until 1903 that Rowlandson's *English Dance of Death* was reissued, and then only in a small private edition. The actual drawings, as distinct from the prints based on them, have (with one or two exceptions) never been reproduced before.

The nineteenth century also saw the development of scholarly interest in the whole topic of the Dance of Death. As already mentioned, the antiquarian Francis Douce supplied a long general introduction on the subject to his edition of Holbein's Dance of Death that first appeared in 1833. This account, many times reissued, has remained a basic source of information, although hosts of later scholars have amplified and refined much of what Douce has to say. The number of books concerned with the Dance of Death has now reached formidable proportions, and there are no indications that the interest of students in the theme is exhausted. Two of the recent publications in the field, both with good bibliographies, are James M. Clark, *The Dance of Death in the Middle Ages and the Renaissance* (Glasgow, 1950), and Edelgard Dubruck, *The Theme of Death in French Poetry of the Middle Ages and the Renaissance* (The Hague, 1964).

III

ROWLANDSON'S DRAWINGS for *The English Dance of Death*, like all his productions, may be enjoyed both in terms of what they represent and as examples of virtuoso draftsmanship. The subject matter of the Dance of Death designs will be sure to hold the attention of anyone curious about the society and manners of early nineteenth-century England. The fact that Rowlandson would take up this theme at all and treat it as he did is in itself an indication of the spirit of the times. The successive reissues of Holbein's Dance of Death during the seventeenth and eighteenth centuries indicate that the public never ceased to be fascinated by the topic. But there is a quickening of the pace in these publications in the late eighteenth and early nineteenth centuries. It may be that the turmoil of the French Revolution and the succeeding Napoleonic Wars stimulated interest in the theme. It may also be that the romantic temperament, which was dominant at the time, found the macabre and grotesque congenial. Whatever the reason, one may safely assume that Rowlandson and Ackermann would not have devoted so much energy to the production of *The English Dance of Death* had they not felt convinced that the work would find a wide audience.

The individual designs, because of the element of fantasy involved, do not always mirror the daily scene with the fidelity of some other Rowlandson drawings, but they are still a very happy hunting ground for the social historian. The appearance of an apothecary's shop, the method of recruiting, the inside of an artist's studio or an insurance office, the way in which skates were fastened to shoes, and endless quantities of data about modes of conveyance: these are only a few of the less likely topics on which the drawings yield helpful information to the curious. And, of course, the whole ritual of death and burial is expounded in ample detail.

For the student of Rowlandson's art, the drawings for *The English Dance of Death* taken together provide probably the most important material we have for an investigation of the various problems connected with the late phase of the artist's work. There are in all about one hundred eighty drawings now known that are clearly related to *The English Dance of Death*. About half of these are together in the Huntington Library, where direct comparative examination is possible. The rest are scattered through various collections, but there are also sizable groups in the New York Public Library and in the Harry Elkins Widener Collection at Harvard. The Huntington cache was obtained in the 1920's from the Philadelphia book dealer Charles Sessler, who in turn had acquired it at the sale of the Bruton collection at Sotheby's on June 10, 1921. Bruton apparently gathered the drawings from various sources, but the bulk of them had belonged to Joseph Parker, who had exhibited them in 1882 at the Burlington Fine Arts Club. Presumably during the time the drawings belonged to Bruton they were mounted and bound by Riviere into two handsome red morocco volumes. These also contain a copy of the published text and designs, together with a complete set of proofs of the etched plates before aquatint, letters, or color were added.

The thirty-three drawings in the Spencer Collection of the New York Public Library also have been together for some time. They were in the Cortland F. Bishop sale at the American Art Association Galleries on November 14, 1938, Lot 1984. The Widener drawings appear to have been acquired from various sources, as were the smaller groups of drawings in other public and private collections.

All the circumstances clearly imply that Rowlandson produced more drawings connected with the series than are at present known. Others will doubtless turn up from time to time, but it is unlikely that their reappearance will make any substantial alteration in the picture of the artist's late technique and methods presented by the group now available.

The one hundred eighty drawings listed in this book represent only ninety-six different subjects. Thus nearly half the drawings are repetitions. Of the seventy-four engraved designs (including frontispiece and title page), drawings are known for all but seven, with frequently three and sometimes as many as five repetitions of the same subject. Rowlandson's repetitions of his drawings remain one of the most vexed and perplexing problems in dealing with his later work, and it is a problem raised emphatically and insistently by the Dance of Death material.

The drawings may be divided into two groups on the basis of size. In one group the drawings usually measure slightly under 5¾ by 9½ inches and are appreciably larger in scale than the prints. In the other the drawings are about an inch smaller in each direction and are much closer to the size of the prints. Drawings of the same subject frequently occur in both sizes and correspond very closely in composition. Several of the drawings, both large and small, retain traces of a grid of pencil lines, suggesting they were squared for transfer. Probably it was by this method that the transition from one size to another was accomplished. The drawings larger in scale are frequently (although not consistently) somewhat freer and broader in treatment than the smaller ones. The designs may have been reduced in size so that they would serve more directly as models in etching the plates. It is much more difficult to suggest any convincing reason why an enlargement would be made from a smaller drawing. Combe's directive to Rowlandson about the alterations in the "Tom Higgins" design occurs on the back of a drawing of the larger scale, indicating that in at least this one instance the larger drawing precedes the preparation for the print. It may be justifiable to conclude that the larger drawings of any particular subject precede the smaller.

The repetitions are related to one another in various ways. The change in scale, as already mentioned, seems to have been accomplished by squaring off the drawings. The remnants of penciled squares and the very close correspondence in placement of details in the related drawings indicate clearly that some such aid must have been employed. Drawings of the same subject that are the same size may have started either as tracings or as counterproofs of one another. The evidence supplied by the Dance of Death drawings concerning Rowlandson's methods of counterproofing is of particular interest (see Figs. 1 and 2). The majority, but not all, of the drawings that are the reverse of the printed designs prove, on close examination, to have started as counterproofs. And in many of these cases the actual drawing is known from which the counterproof was pulled. Drawings that started as counterproofs have normally been strengthened or reinforced, presumably by the artist himself. Occasionally the original drawing has also been reinforced after the counterproof was pulled.

The visual evidence concerning Rowlandson's methods is given strong corroboration by an account of his use of counterproofing given in *Notes and Queries*, Series 4, Volume IV, page 89. This article, which ap-

FIG. 1. *Detail of 15a.*

FIG. 2. *Detail of 15b. A partially reworked counterproof pulled from 15a. Note that some lines were added to 15a after the counterproof was pulled (see Introduction, p. 15).*

peared in 1869, is signed only "W. P." Apparently the same "W. P." also contributed articles on Rudolph Ackermann to *Notes and Queries* in the same year. The *Dictionary of National Biography* article on Ackermann identifies the author of the latter notes as Wyatt Papworth, the younger son of J. B. Papworth, who was closely associated with Ackermann. The account of the counterproofing technique is reasonably well known but is certainly worth quoting in full:

> If at any time collectors should be surprised at finding that five or six of his [Rowlandson's] productions are almost exactly similar in outline, and scarcely different in colour, they may rest assured that all are by him, and were considered by him to be equally originals. The process of production was simple. Rowlandson would call in the Strand, ask for paper, vermilion, a brush, water, a saucer, and a reed; then, making of the reed such a pen as he liked, he drew the outline of a subject (generally taking care to reverse the arms of his figures), and handed the paper to Mr. Ackermann to be treated as if it were a copper-plate. This was taken to the press, where some well-damped paper was laid upon the sketch, and the two were subjected to a pressure that turned them out as a right and left outline. The operation would be performed with other pieces of damp paper in succession, until the original would not part with vermilion enough to indicate an outline; then that original became useless, and Rowlandson proceeded to reline the replicas, and to tint them according to the fancy of the moment.

The drawings at hand for *The English Dance of Death* confirm beyond doubt that some sort of counterproofing process similar to the one described by W. P. must have been used by Rowlandson. But there are some details in the account that are not fully borne out by the evidence. In no instance has more than one counterproof been located that has clearly been pulled from the same drawing. It seems, in fact, improbable that several counterproofs could be taken from one original. Also, contrary to W. P.'s statement, Rowlandson was not always careful about reversing details in the original drawings. In several instances letters on various signs in the drawings are permitted to remain in reverse on the counterproof. But the basic point, that Rowlandson himself made counterproofs of his drawings, seems clearly established by the evidence. The counterproofs surely must have been made while the ink was still damp. The fact that the original drawings were frequently retouched after the counterproof was pulled tends further to confirm that the reproductions were made by the artist himself.

The draftsmanship involved in the drawings varies considerably, not only in quality but in a more purely calligraphic sense as well. There are three principal types of lines that are found in the drawings (see Figs. 3, 4, 5, and 6). The most prevalent of these is a comparatively flexible line normally in a reddish black ink. The second is a much tighter and more uniform line, sometimes in black but also frequently in vermilion. The character of this line, as well as the context in which it normally appears, strongly implies that it is a tracing line, or at least a line made by copying from another drawing. It is neat and workmanlike but lacks the freedom and flexibility of the first. The third line is very coarse and is used to reinforce the shadow areas of the figures. It is usually in vermilion and is found frequently on drawings where the initial outline is of the comparatively tight uniform variety. But it also occurs on drawings executed primarily in the first type of line. Like the first type of line, the third is much freer and more flexible in character than the second. All three lines often occur in one drawing; nor is the distinction, especially between the first two, always clear-cut.

The second type of line is one that by mid-twentieth-century criteria of connoisseurship we would be inclined to attribute to an assistant or a copyist. This interpretation may be correct, but we should also be cautious about applying our own standards to a different period. Clearly Rowlandson did duplicate his own work by copying as well as counterproofing. For this we have the unassailable contemporary evidence provided by the title page of the catalog of Rowlandson's sale at Sotheby's in June of 1828, which included drawings of "several of his most celebrated subjects, many of them the originals from which he made duplicate drawings." It is also apparent from the drawings themselves that he preferred semimechanical methods of reproduction (tracings and counterproofs) rather than free-style copies and variants.

There are in the Ashmolean Museum four drawings for *The English Dance of Death* that are of great interest in any discussion of the problem of repetitions and copies of Rowlandson's designs. The four drawings were bequeathed to the Bodleian by the antiquarian Francis Douce in 1834. On the old mount of one of the drawings there is a penciled inscription that reads: "Copy by Miss Howitt." (See Nos. 13b, 15c, 61b, 92c.)

Paul Oppé, in his 1923 book on Rowlandson, appears to have been the first student to take proper note of these drawings and the inscription. He thought the inscription was by Douce himself, who was certainly in a position to know what he had. Oppé accordingly attributed the drawings to Miss Howitt, although he said in effect that were it not for the inscription they might readily pass as undistinguished repetitions by Rowlandson himself. Miss Howitt was thought to be the daughter of Rowlandson's brother-in-law, the draftsman Samuel Howitt. The inscription is the only refer-

FIG. 3. *Detail of 3a, showing first type of line.*

FIG. 4. *Detail of 3c, showing line two reinforced by line one. A reduced copy, the outlines considerably reinforced (see Introduction, pp. 18-19).*

FIG. 5. *Detail of 10a, showing line one.*

FIG. 6. *Detail of 10b, showing line one reinforced by line three. Probably began as a tracing from 10a. Note the coarse but flexible reinforcing lines (see Introduction, pp. 18-19).*

ence known giving the name of one of Rowlandson's assistants; indeed it is the only documentary evidence we have that he employed assistants.

The four Ashmolean drawings are executed throughout in the second type of line with no noticeable reinforcement from the other two. If this line could be established as definitely by Miss Howitt, a whole avenue for dealing with late drawings by Rowlandson would be thrown open.

But unfortunately the evidence concerning the drawings is far from clear. All four are repetitions; stronger versions of all of them are known; one of the Ashmolean drawings actually began as a counterproof. Nevertheless, three of them are signed with authentic-looking Rowlandson signatures, and one of the drawings bears an inscription that is certainly in Rowlandson's own hand.

As an additional complication, investigation reveals that the inscription designating one drawing as "copy by Miss Howitt" is probably not in Douce's handwriting. Furthermore, Douce did make two definite statements about the drawings, both indicating that he thought they were by Rowlandson. He apparently purchased them in 1826 (the year before Rowlandson's death), and the entry in his manuscript "List of Antiquarian Purchases" reads under 1826: "4 drawings of a D. dance by Rowlandson. Of Howitt." It is highly interesting that the name Howitt should appear in this notation. But the other entries in the account book leave little room to doubt that the proper interpretation of the note is that the drawings were by Rowlandson, purchased from someone by the name of Howitt. Who this might be we do not know. Samuel Howitt was already dead, and it seems unlikely that Douce would refer to a Miss Howitt simply by her surname.

Douce also speaks of the drawings in the long introduction to his edition of Holbein's Dance of Death, published in 1833, and he there writes of them as by Rowlandson, with no reference to anyone by the name of Howitt. There seems, in fact, no reason to doubt that Douce himself accepted the drawings as by Rowlandson. And so the whole theory, based on his authority, that they are the work of Miss Howitt, tends to collapse, and with it our one shred of documentary evidence concerning Rowlandson's assistants. The inscription still remains, but being now anonymous and undated, it cannot be given much weight. It may have been added by someone who, recognizing the patently inferior quality of the drawings, wishfully misinterpreted the entry in Douce's account book.

At best the four drawings are no more than weak repetitions. Simply on the basis of appearance the wish to classify them as the work of an assistant is readily understandable. But unfortunately it is equally plausible to put a different interpretation on the visual and other evidence. We know that Rowlandson made copies of his drawings, but we do not know what changes his own draftsmanship would undergo in these circumstances. The very facts that Douce bought the Ashmolean drawings during Rowlandson's lifetime as the work of that artist and that he was sufficiently confident of that attribution to publish a description of them in which he has no hesitation in presenting them as Rowlandson's work are strong arguments for accepting them. The conclusion then would be that Rowlandson in duplicating his own designs becomes much more mechanical than in the initial drawings.

There are many circumstances that affect the appearance of the lines in the drawings. The lines in those sketches that began as counterproofs, or from which counterproofs have been pulled, normally have a "sucked out" appearance. The contrast with the surrounding paper has been softened, with the result that the drawing as a whole lacks sparkle. The presence of reinforcing lines on many of the drawings, applied with different pen and ink from the basic outlines, gives these examples a more complex appearance, which again dilutes their visual vitality. And, of course, the tight, wiry lines that normally occur in the repetitions lack the ease, flexibility, and assurance of the lines in the prototypes. Thus differences in quality unquestionably exist: some drawings have great freshness and vigor; others are tired and mechanical. Much as we might like to, however, it would be an unjustifiable simplification to dismiss the less good drawings as the work of assistants. There may be other hands involved in the repetitions. Rowlandson may have employed helpers to copy his outlines, which he then reinforced in varying degrees himself. But there is at present no clear evidence to support this assumption, aside from our reluctance to allow that a distinguished artist could be a dull copyist of his own work.

Joseph Grego, that indefatigable student of Rowlandson whose two volumes on the artist remain our fullest source of information about his work, speaks of *The English Dance of Death* as containing "a selection from Rowlandson's famous illustrations" for the subject. It would appear that this is no idle phrase and that Grego, as usual, knew what he was talking about. There are many drawings known that from their subjects, style, format, and physical size are clearly connected with the series but were not included among the published designs. Twenty-eight of these additional drawings have been located and are included in the present book. There is no reason to suppose that this exhausts the supply; others doubtless remain to be discovered. There has been no attempt, however, to include every design by Rowlandson in which Death or a skeleton is present but only those which may be reasonably considered, on the basis of subject, style, and physical dimensions, as forming part of the *English Dance of Death* series.

As the number of designs to be used in the publication was fixed from the outset, the most likely explanation for the additional drawings is that Rowlandson offered Combe a choice. Several of the unused designs nearly duplicate subjects in the published series; they may be alternative compositions. Others involve subjects that would not offer appropriate scope for Combe's "metrical illustrations." Still others may have been undertaken simply for Rowlandson's own amusement.

There are fewer repetitions among the drawings that were not engraved, but some exist. Interestingly enough, however, there do not appear to be any counterproofs. This fact may imply that the counterproofs are in some way connected with preparing the designs for the etcher. On the other hand there is ample evidence that the printmakers working for Ackermann were in complete command of means for producing an impression that would not be the reverse of any given design. Most of the unused designs are in the larger format, but not invariably so.

The Dance of Death drawings form a fascinating and instructive contrast with the other major Rowlandson series in the Huntington collection, the drawings for a Tour in a Post Chaise. If *The English Dance of Death* is among the last of Rowlandson's important achievements, the Tour in a Post Chaise is among the first. The early series dates almost certainly from 1784, when Rowlandson was still in his twenties and had just achieved artistic recognition. The second series is thirty years later. The first is the record of an actual trip, with surprisingly accurate attention to topographical and other details along the route. The second is largely the product of Rowlandson's imagination. The Tour was never published in the artist's own day, and one suspects it was undertaken primarily for his own satisfaction. The Dance of Death was surely a commercial undertaking from the outset. One is an autograph document, and very few copies of any of the drawings are known; the other immediately involves us in the tangled web of Rowlandson's studio practice and his methods of duplicating his designs.

The contrast between the two sets of drawings from the visual and technical points of view is equally interesting. The early drawings are relatively uncomplicated. The color is applied in simple washes, and the contours are defined by penwork which is both much more consistent and much more flexible from the purely calligraphic standpoint than that in the later work. In the later series the application of color has become more sophisticated. Color is used more for modeling, with washes applied over one another. Likewise, the calligraphic treatment is more involved, with different types of penwork employed to achieve what Rowlandson had earlier accomplished with one more versatile line.

There can be little doubt concerning which is the more attractive of the two series (at least to mid-twentieth-century eyes). But there can also be little doubt that our understanding of Rowlandson's personality would be distinctly incomplete and lopsided if we did not take both series into account. The repetitions and copies that betray what to modern judgment is a casual attitude toward his work, the frequent lapses into crude and vulgar themes that pander to the lowest levels of human taste—these are unquestionably present in the later series and are parts of Rowlandson's personal makeup that cannot be ignored. But the Dance of Death drawings also attest to the almost incredible fertility of Rowlandson's imagination, which was never richer and more original. And the best of the drawings retain a command and vigor that are worthy of Rowlandson's astonishing gifts as a draftsman.

DRAWINGS FOR *THE ENGLISH DANCE OF DEATH*

FRONTISPIECE

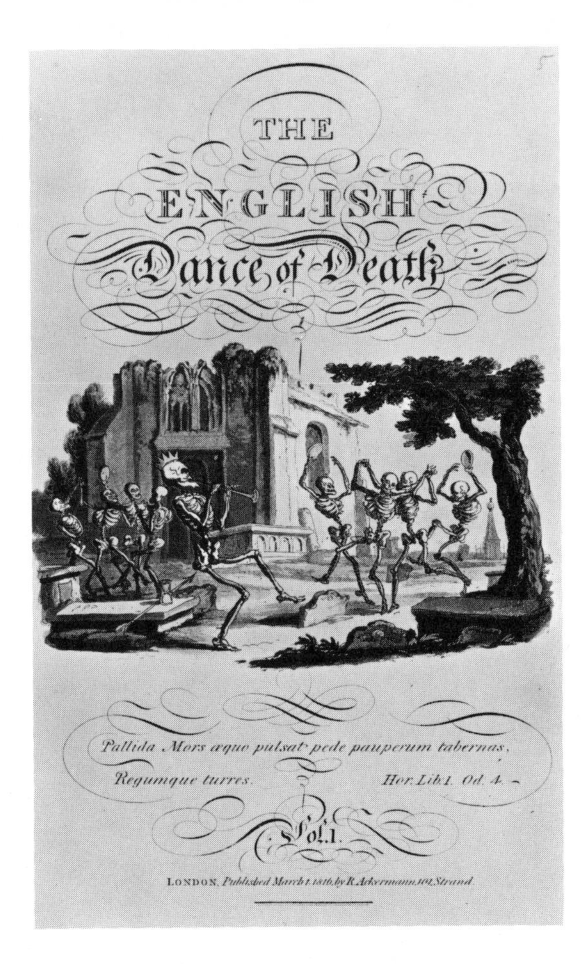

THE

ENGLISH

Dance of Death

Pallida Mors æquo pulsat pede pauperum tabernas,

Regumque turres. *Hor. Lib. 1. Od. 4.*

Vol. 1.

LONDON, *Published March 1. 1816, by R. Ackermann, 101, Strand.*

TITLE PAGE

1. TIME AND DEATH

2. THE ANTIQUARY'S LAST WILL & TESTAMENT

3. THE LAST CHASE

4. THE STATESMAN

5. TOM HIGGINS

6. THE SHIPWRECK

7. THE VIRAGO

8. THE GLUTTON

9. THE RECRUIT

10. THE MAIDEN LADIES

11. THE QUACK DOCTOR

12. THE SOT

13. THE HONEY MOON

14. THE HUNTER UNKENNELLED

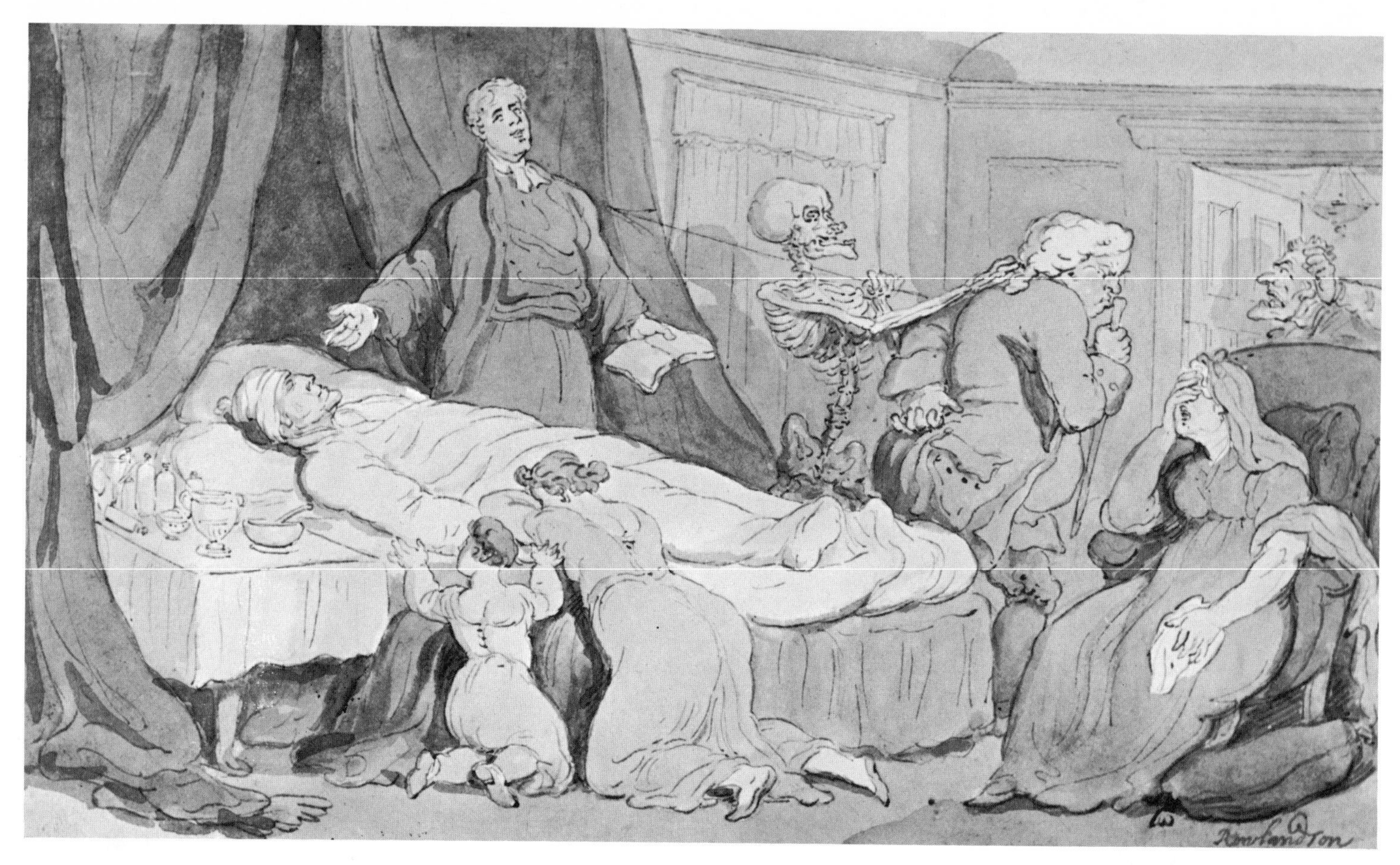

15. THE GOOD MAN, DEATH, AND THE DOCTOR

16. DEATH AND THE PORTRAIT

17. THE GENEALOGIST

18. THE CATCHPOLE

19. THE INSURANCE OFFICE

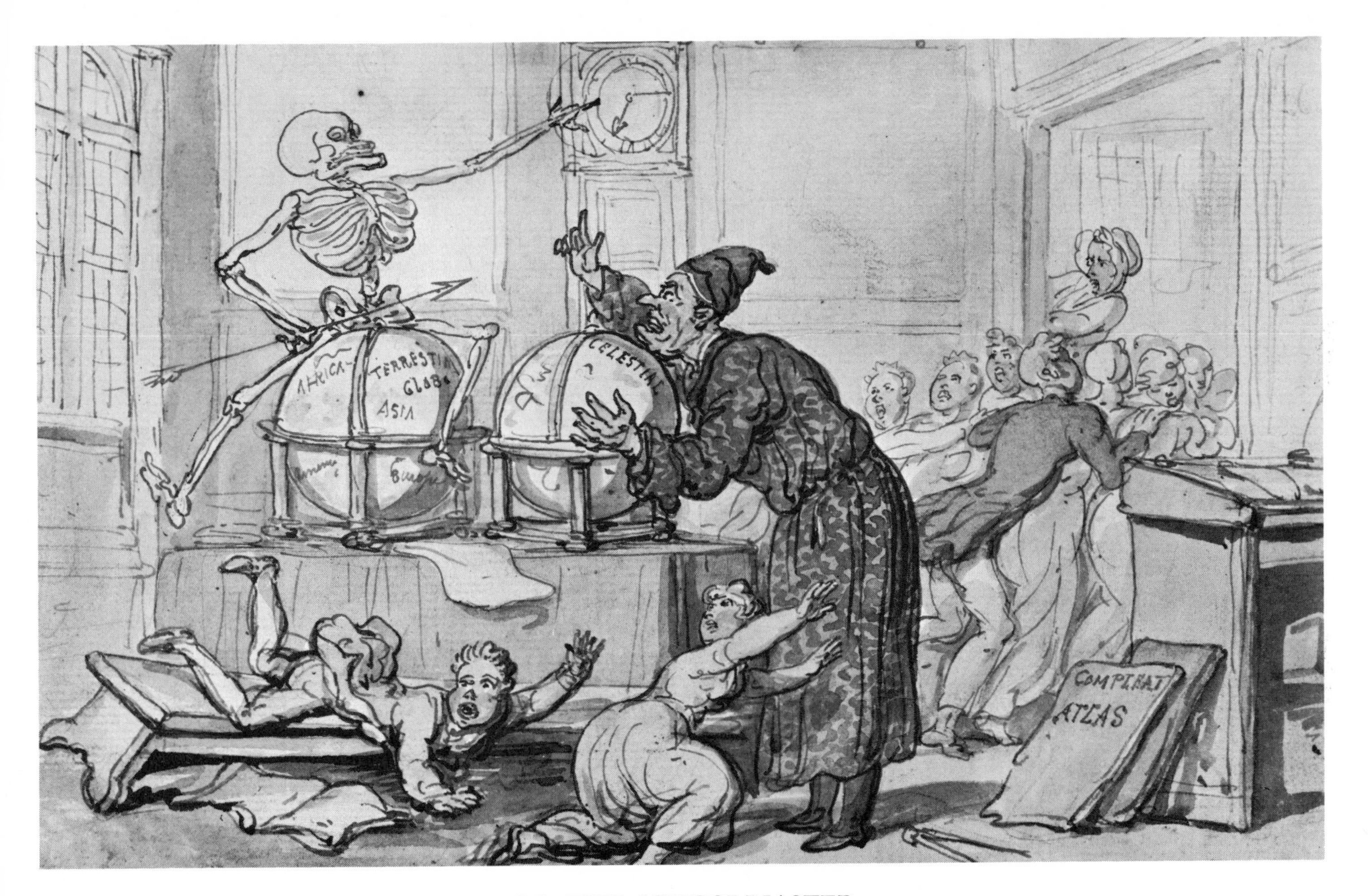

20. THE SCHOOLMASTER

21. THE COQUETTE

22. TIME & DEATH, AND GOODY BARTON

23. THE UNDERTAKER & THE QUACK

24. THE MASQUERADE *(proof before aquatint)*

25. THE DEATH BLOW

26. THE VISION OF SKULLS

27. THE PORTER'S CHAIR

28. THE PANTOMIME

29. THE HORSE RACE

30. THE DRAM SHOP

31. THE GAMING TABLE

32. THE BATTLE

33. THE WEDDING *(colored proof before aquatint)*

34. THE SKAITERS

35. THE DUEL

36. THE BISHOP AND DEATH

37. THE SUICIDE

38. CHAMPAGNE, SHERRY, AND WATER GRUEL

39. THE NURSERY

40. THE ASTRONOMER

41. THE FATHER OF THE FAMILY

42. THE FALL OF FOUR IN HAND

43. GAFFER GOODMAN

44. THE URCHIN ROBBERS

45. DEATH TURNED PILOT

46. THE WINDING UP OF THE CLOCK

47. THE FAMILY OF CHILDREN

48. DEATH'S DOOR

49. THE FIRE

50. THE MISER'S END

51. GRETNA GREEN

52. THE WALTZ

53. MATERNAL TENDERNESS *(proof before aquatint)*

54. THE KITCHEN

55. THE GIG

56. THE MAUSOLEUM

57. THE COURTSHIP

58. THE TOASTMASTER

59. THE CARELESS AND THE CAREFUL *(print)*

60. THE LAW OVERTHROWN

61. THE FORTUNE TELLER

62. THE LOTTERY OFFICE *(proof before aquatint)*

63. THE PRISONER DISCHARGED

64. THE GALLANT'S DOWNFALL

65. THE CHURCH YARD DEBATE

66. THE GOOD AND GREAT *(print)*

67. THE NEXT HEIR

68. THE CHAMBER WAR

69. DEATH AND THE ANTIQUARIES

70. THE DAINTY DISH

71. THE LAST STAGE

72. TIME, DEATH, AND ETERNITY

73. THE MAN OF FEELING

74. THE OLD SUITOR REJECTED

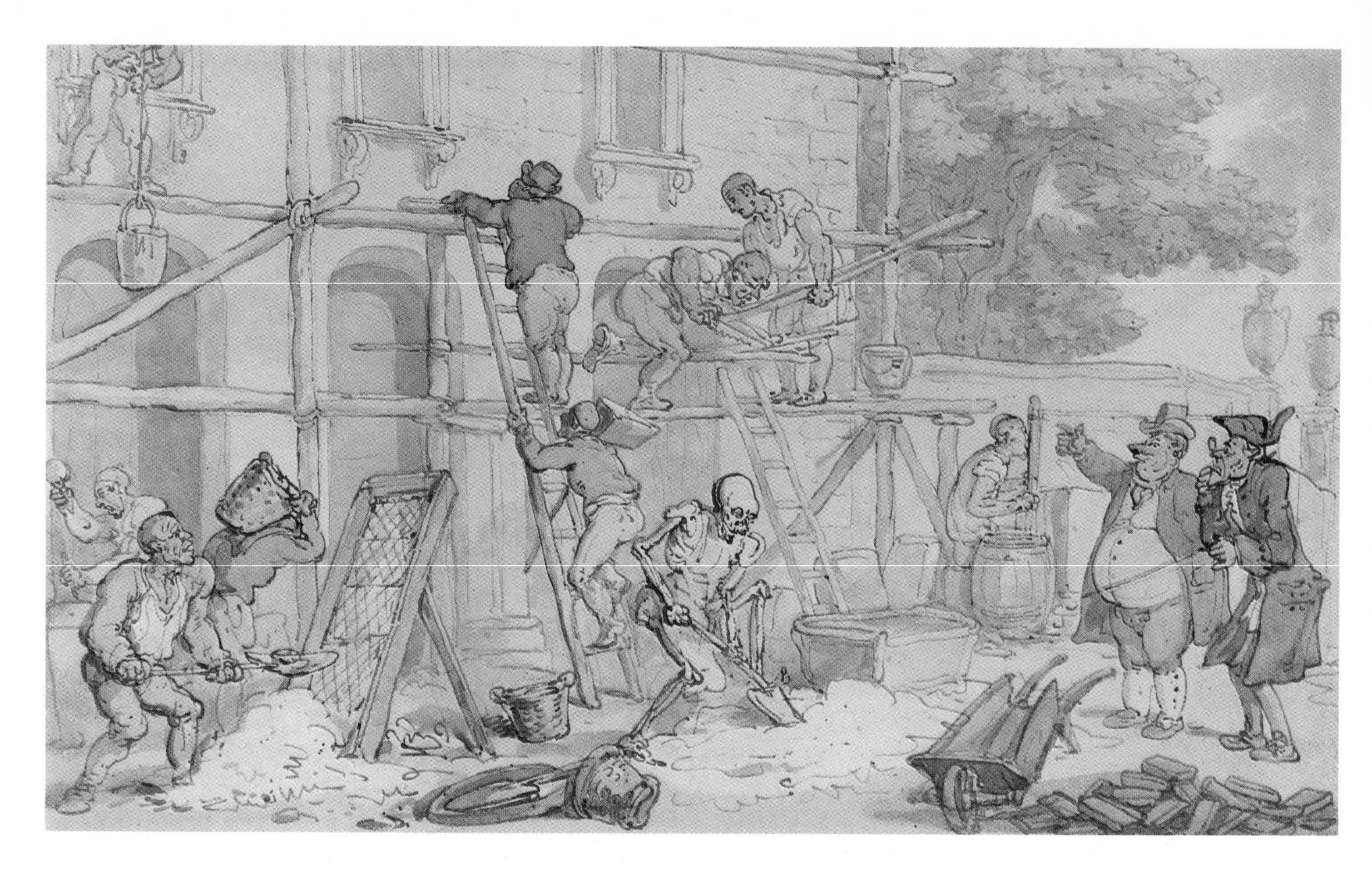

75. DEATH MIXING THE MORTAR

76. DEATH AT THE DOOR

77. THE SWORD DUEL

78. THE YOUNG FAMILY MOURNING IN THE CHURCHYARD

79. DEATH IN A BALLROOM

80. DEATH HELPING AN OLD LOVER INTO BED

81. RELEASED FROM DEATH

82. DEATH AND THE BUTCHER

83. THE BARBER SHOP

84. THE PUMP ROOM DOOR

85. DEATH AS POSTILION

86. THE OLD LADY AFIRE

87. DEATH IN THE DISSECTION ROOM

88. DEATH GARROTING A PRISONER

89. DEATH AND THE HIGHWAYMAN

90. DEATH AND THE DOCTOR LEAVING THE SICKROOM

91. DEATH ENTERING A SICKROOM THROUGH A WINDOW

92. THE GAMESTER'S EXIT

93. DEATH PULLING A FAT MAN IN A WHEELCHAIR

94. NAILING THE COFFIN

95. THE ASSASSINATION

96. DEATH REJOICING AT A NAVAL BATTLE

97. DEATH AND THE KNIGHT

98. DEATH AND THE DEBAUCHEE

99. THE PRISONER'S MEAL

100. DEATH AND THE NABOB

CATALOG OF THE DRAWINGS FOR *THE ENGLISH DANCE OF DEATH*

Note on the Catalog

Abbreviations used in the text:

HEH—Henry E. Huntington Library and Art Gallery

NYP—The Spencer Collection in the New York Public Library

HCL—The Harry Elkins Widener Collection in the Harvard College Library

Inscriptions on the drawings are in Rowlandson's hand unless otherwise stated. The handwritten labels mounted with (but not actually on) many of the drawings are probably but not indubitably in Rowlandson's hand. No attempt has been made to retain all the eccentricities of printing, capitalization, and punctuation in transcribing the inscriptions. In the descriptions of the prints the information given in italics is taken from the plates.

The asterisk indicates the drawing (or, in a few instances, the print) that is illustrated.

FRONTISPIECE

PRINT:

No date, presumably prepared to accompany the completed two volumes, issued on March 1, 1816. 7 1/16 x 4¼ in.

Proof before aquatint: the open book is blank. First state: no aquatint on the America section of the globe.

DRAWING:

* HEH: 7⅛ x 4¼ in.; pen and watercolor, with preliminary pencil work. There is no lettering on the globe. The labels on the containers are not all the same as in the print: read "gin" for "compounds," "phisic" for "drugs."

The image of Death seated on a globe may be an inverted reminiscence of "The Last Judgment" in Holbein's Dance of Death. Christ there sits on a rainbow resting His feet on a globe of the universe.

A frontispiece with Death crowned, seated on a throne, occurs in *Schau-Platz des Todes, oder Todten-Tanz*, by Salomon Van Rusting (Nuremberg, 1736).

TITLE PAGE

*PRINT:

London, Published March 1, 1816, by R. Ackermann, 101, Strand.
Approx. 3¼ x 5⅜ in. (without letters).

There is in the Huntington Library a proof before aquatint and letters, on Whatman paper dated 1812.

DRAWINGS:

No drawings for this subject are known.

The subject of the dead dancing in a churchyard is not a part of the regular Dance of Death. It derives from an independent source concerned with the legend that the dead rise from their graves at night and dance, attempting to entice the living to join them. But the appearance of the subject in the Dance of Death is not particularly unusual. Holbein included it as Pl. V.

1. TIME AND DEATH

PRINT:

London, Pub. 1 April 1814 by R. Ackermann, 101 Strand.

Time & Death their Thoughts impart
On Works of Learning & of Art

4 15/16 x 8 5/16 in.

First state: no aquatint on the open book lying on the floor in the foreground. The normal color scheme has the historian's coat purple, Time's robe blue, the artist's coat and the tablecloth green. The HEH impression of the first state has the historian's coat blue, Time's green, and the artist's brown.

DRAWINGS:

*(a) HEH: 5 13/16 x 9⅜ in.; pen and watercolor, squared off in pencil; inscribed "Time and Death outwitted by the Historian and Painter"; the bowl to the right inscribed "Medals/Coins"; many minor variations from the print, especially in the rows of busts.

(b) NYP: 4 15/16 x 8 7/16 in.; pen and watercolor. There are still minor variations from the print, but this drawing is closer to the print than is (a).

(c) Glasgow Art Gallery: 5 15/16 x 9 9/16 in.; pen and watercolor, unfinished; bears the same inscriptions as (a); many minor variations from the print and the other drawings. Probably began as a tracing from (a), or vice versa.

This subject does not appear in other treatments of the Dance of Death; Rowlandson's use of it in this context appears to be original. The fact that Rowlandson both begins and ends his series with designs depicting the defeat of Death and Time helps to lighten the whole effect and makes the humor with which he treats his sinister theme more palatable.

The scene is slightly reminiscent of Zoffany's well-known painting of Charles Towneley and his friends surrounded by Towneley's collection of ancient marbles. The Towneley marbles were acquired by the British Museum in 1805 and placed on display in a newly constructed gallery in 1808. His bronzes, coins, gems, and drawings were acquired by the museum in 1814.

2. THE ANTIQUARY'S LAST WILL & TESTAMENT

PRINT:

London, Pub. 1 April 1814, at R. Ackermann's, 101 Strand.

Fungus, at length, contrives to get Death's Dart into his Cabinet.

4¾ x 8¼ in.

Proof before aquatint: the scroll in the foreground is inscribed "Bills of / Mortality"; one container is labeled "Crucible." First state: the word "mortality" alone appears on a scroll in the foreground; it is largely obscured by heavier aquatint in the later states. The normal color scheme has the bed canopy green and the chair behind Death purple.

DRAWINGS:

*(a) HEH: 5 11/16 x 9 5/16 in.; pen and watercolor, with considerable reinforcement in sanguine; squared off in pencil. Lettered on the drawing: "Almanack" (behind Death's dart); "Maps / Charts" (between bed and table); "Algebra" (book open on bed). Mounted with the drawing is a handwritten label with the title "The Antiquarian and Death" followed by the same caption that appears on the print.

(b) Achenbach Foundation for Graphic Arts, California Palace of the Legion of Honor: 5⅝ x 9 3/16 in.; pen and watercolor; numerous variations from the print, the most important being that the skeleton of Death is seen hanging in the closet to the left, where the armor is placed in the print. Strictly speaking, the drawing is thus not a Dance of Death subject.

(c) HEH: 4 13/16 x 8 9/16 in.; pen (sanguine) and watercolor; squared off in pencil, the position of the lines corresponding to those in (a); signed, lower left, "Rowlandson."

(d) HCL: in reverse; 4⅞ x 8 7/16 in.; pen and watercolor; probably began as a counterproof pulled from (c).

Bills of Mortality, which figure in the print, were returns published weekly by the London Company of Parish Clerks, recording the deaths (and later also the births) for the 109 parishes in and around London. The practice began in the 1530's and continued until 1842, when it was superseded by the registrar-general's returns. In the early eighteenth century ages of the dead were introduced, thus making the bills of considerable statistical value.

3. THE LAST CHASE

PRINT:

London, Pub. 1 April 1814, by R. Ackermann, 101 Strand.

Such mortal Sport the Chase attends:
At Break-Neck Hill, the Hunting Ends.

4 13/16 x 8 1/16 in.

First state: no aquatint on the bank behind the fore-legs of Death's horse. Second state: the aquatint cloud behind Death is still undeveloped. The normal color scheme has blue for the coat of the falling horseman, brownish-red for the coat of the horseman reining in. A colored proof before aquatint is in HCL.

DRAWINGS:

*(a) HEH: 5 11/16 x 9¼ in.; pen and watercolor with some preliminary pencil.

(b) HEH: 5¾ x 9 5/16 in.; pen and watercolor with reinforcement in sanguine; squared off in pencil. A more highly finished and much tighter drawing than (a); apparently traced, at least in general outline, from (a).

(c) HEH: 4¾ x 8 7/16 in.; pen (sanguine) and watercolor; signed, lower right, "Rowlandson"; squared off in pencil, the positions of the lines corresponding to those in (b); mounted with the drawing is a handwritten label with the title "The Last Chase" followed by the same caption that appears on the print.

(d) HCL: in reverse; 5 x 8⅛ in.; pen and watercolor; certainly began as a counterproof, possibly derived from (c).

The idea of death involved in a fall from a horse or a carriage (one of the commonest hazards of the day) seems to have had a particular interest for Rowlandson. Variations on the theme occur in six of the published designs.

4. THE STATESMAN

PRINT:

London, Pub. May 1, 1814 at R. Ackermann's, 101 Strand.

Not all the Statesman's power or art
Can turn aside Death's certain Dart.

4¾ x 8 7/16 in.

First state: the group of small smudges to the right of the statesman's face is absent. Second state: the hands of the clock are not completely covered by the aquatint ground. The normal color scheme has purple for the settee, green for the floor and tablecloth, brown for the statesman's coat.

DRAWINGS:

*(a) HEH: 5 13/16 x 9 5/16 in.; pen and watercolor, with traces of preparatory pencil; squared off in pencil; inscribed "This Man sold his Country for Gold"; the chart inscribed "Cornish Burrows Bought / and sold / Grampound / Camelford / St. Austle / St. Micheal / St.—"; the sign next inscribed "Sinecures / Promotions / Patronage / Presenta / tions"; the box in the foreground labeled "Secure / Votes" and "Box of / Bribery / and / Corruption." The bust is labeled "Midas." Mounted with the drawing is a handwritten

label with the title "The Statesman" followed by the same caption that appears with the print.

(b) HEH: 5 x 8 7/16 in.; pen and watercolor with traces of preparatory pencil; remnants of pencil lines corresponding to squares on (a); the chart is labeled "Canal Shares," the sign beneath the clock, "Game Laws." Background is much closer to the print than in (a).

(c) HEH: 4 15/16 x 8½ in.; pen and watercolor; signed, lower right, "Rowlandson"; chart on the wall inscribed "County of Cornwall / Rotten Bouroughs / Grampound / Camelford / Bodmin"; the sign beneath the clock, "Bribery / Corruption / Plunder." There are many minor variations from the print. A weak drawing; the line lacks the ease and assurance of (a) and (b); the wash is muddy.

(d) NYP: in reverse; 4 15/16 x 8⅛ in.; pen and wash; started as a counterproof derived from (b). Note in particular the inscriptions in reverse corresponding to those in (b).

The references on the drawings (omitted in the print and Combe's verses) to Cornish rotten boroughs are of topical interest. Grampound, Camelford, and Bodmin were notorious rotten boroughs. The towns of St. Austell and St. Michael in Cornwall did not actually return members. There was an investigation of Cornish elections resulting in an important trial at Bodmin in August 1808, fully reported by William Cobbett in his *Weekly Political Register*. It is just possible that Rowlandson may have in mind Andrew James Cochrane Johnstone, who represented Grampound at the time, having expended enormous bribes for his seat. He was involved in shady stock speculations in February of 1814 and was tried for conspiracy in June but managed to escape from the country. (See W. P. Courtney, *The Parliamentary Representation of Cornwall to 1832* [London, 1889], p. 198, and article in the *Dictionary of National Biography* on Johnstone.)

5. TOM HIGGINS

PRINT:

London, Pub. May 1, 1814 by R. Ackermann, 101, Strand.

His blood is stopp'd in ev'ry vein,
He ne'er will eat or drink again.

4⅝ x 8 5/16 in.

First state: no continuous band of aquatint underlining the paunch of Tom Higgins. The normal color scheme has Higgins' coat blue and his waistcoat yellow. The early states may have the coat buff and the waistcoat rust.

DRAWINGS:

*(a) HEH: 5 11/16 x 9¼ in.; pen and watercolor; remnants of preliminary pencil; squared off in pencil; inscribed in pencil on verso in Combe's hand: "(6) a man asleep could [illegible] change [illegible] red cap for a wig & his slippers for shoes, it would suit me better. If he were a little better dressed and more as if he were an Esquire I should be glad."

(b) Philip Hofer: 5⅞ x 9½ in.; pen and watercolor; close to (a), still with cap and slippers.

(c) NYP: 4⅝ x 8½ in.; pen and watercolor; squared off in pencil, the positions of the lines corresponding to those in (a); close to the print; the changes requested by Combe have been made.

The pencil inscription on the verso of (a) is the only explicit indication of Combe's requesting a modification in a drawing for the sake of his story.

6. THE SHIPWRECK

PRINT:

London, Pub. May 1, 1814 at R. Ackermann's, 101 Strand.

The Dangers of the Ocean Oer,
Death Wrecks the Sailors on the Shore.

4¾ x 8 7/16 in.

First state: no aquatint on the sailors' feet or on the sand along the bottom margin. The normal color scheme has the sailor with head on his hands in blue, the other in blue-striped trousers. There is a colored proof before aquatint in the Huntington Library, signed "Rowlandson." Mounted with this print is a handwritten label with the title "The Shipwreck" followed by the caption that appears on the normal issues of the print.

DRAWINGS:

*(a) HEH: 5⅝ x 9¼ in.; pen and watercolor; clear indications of pencil beneath, but apparently not squared off.

(b) NYP: in reverse; 4 11/16 x 8¼ in.; clearly began as a counterproof (note the lines of the masts and of the rock on which Death sits), but not derived from (a).

Combe, in his verses, gives the ship that is wrecked the name of "Lapwing." There does not appear to have been any vessel of that name lost at the time, and it is doubtful if Rowlandson intended any specific reference.

7. THE VIRAGO

PRINT:

London, Pub. June 1, 1814 at R. Ackermann's, 101 Strand.

Her tongue & temper to subdue:
Can only be perform'd by you.

4½ x 7 15/16 in.

First state: no aquatint on immediate foreground. The normal color scheme has the virago's dress green, her shawl pink, and her spouse's robe purple.

DRAWINGS:

* *(a) HEH: 5¾ x 9 7/16 in.; pen and watercolor; squared off in pencil; inscribed "The Happy release or Tranquility Restored."

(b) HEH: 4 7/16 x 8 in.; pen and watercolor, reinforced in sanguine; squared off in pencil, the positions of the lines corresponding to those in (a); mounted with the drawing is a handwritten label with the title "The Virago" followed by the same caption that appears on the print.

The theme of Death and the henpecked husband occurs in *Den Algemeynen Dooden Spiegel van Pater Abraham à Sancta Clara* (Brussels, 1730) and also in Newton's Dances of Death (London, 1796).

8. THE GLUTTON

PRINT:

London, Pub. June 1, 1814 at R. Ackermann's, 101 Strand.

What do these sav'ry meats delight you?
Begone, & stay, till I invite you.

4⅝ x 7⅞ in.

First state: no aquatint on the floor bordering the fallen chair. The normal color scheme calls for the two chairs to be green and the glutton's suit brown.

DRAWINGS:

* *(a) HEH: 5⅝ x 9¼ in.; pen and watercolor; squared off in pencil.

(b) Philip Hofer: 5⅞ x 9½ in.; pen and watercolor; several minor differences; not so close to the print as (a); inscribed "Rowlandson" (does not appear to be a genuine signature).

(c) HCL: 5½ x 9 in.; pen and watercolor; close to (b).

(d) NYP: 4¼ x 7 13/16 in.; pen and watercolor with vermilion reinforcement; squared off in pencil, the positions of the lines corresponding to those in (a); close to (a) and the print.

(e) Philip Hofer: in reverse; 4⅝ x 8 in.; pen and watercolor; signed "Rowlandson"; probably began as a counterproof, but apparently not pulled from any of the other known drawings. Mounted with the drawing is a handwritten label with the title "The Glutton" followed by the same caption that appears on the print.

The theme of Death and the glutton appears in J. R. Schellenberg's *Freund Heins Erscheinungen in Holbeins Manier* (Winterthur, 1785).

9. THE RECRUIT

PRINT:

London, Pub. June 1, 1814 at R. Ackermann's, 101 Strand.

I list you, and you'll soon be found,
One of my regiment under ground.

4½ x 7⅝ in.

First state: the figure on crutches has a line across his chest that is not reinforced with aquatint. The normal color scheme has the girl's dress pink, her apron and the recruit's trousers blue. There is a proof with grisaille wash in HCL.

DRAWINGS:

*(a) HEH: 5 11/16 x 9½ in.; pen and watercolor; squared off in pencil.

(b) HEH: in reverse; 4 7/16 x 7 9/16 in.; pen and watercolor; signed "Rowlandson." Mounted with the drawing is a handwritten label with the title "The Recruit" followed by the same caption that appears on the print. The drawing has been worked over throughout but fairly clearly began as a counterproof.

The print appeared while Europe was briefly at peace during Napoleon's exile on Elba. The subject would thus seem a little less sinister than at a time of active recruiting with a military campaign in progress. The theme of Death enlisting some country fellows occurs in J. R. Schellenberg, *Freund Heins Erscheinungen in Holbeins Manier* (Winterthur, 1785).

10. THE MAIDEN LADIES

PRINT:

London, Pub. July 1, 1814 at R. Ackermann's, 101 Strand.

Be not alarm'd:—I'm only come
To choose a wife, & light her home.

4¾ x 8⅛ in.

First state: the shadow of the monkey barely reaches the elbow of the prostrate woman. The normal color scheme has the table top and curtains green, the footman's coat yellow, and his waistcoat blue.

DRAWINGS:

*(a) HEH: 5 11/16 x 9¼ in.; pen and watercolor; squared off in pencil; the verso is also squared in pencil, the lines being in the same position as those on the front. Several of the squares on the verso are numbered.

(b) HEH: 5¾ x 9 5/16 in.; pen and watercolor, with some heavy reinforcement in sanguine, especially in the fallen figure and the monkey in the left foreground. Probably the two drawings are related through tracing, but the sequence is not clear.

11. THE QUACK DOCTOR

PRINT:

London, Pub. July 1, 1814 at R. Ackermann's, 101 Strand.

I have a secret art to cure
Each malady, which men endure.

4⅞ x 7 15/16 in.

First state: no aquatint on the left calf of the seated man. The normal color scheme has the quack's suit purple, the seated man's coat blue, and the curtain green.

DRAWINGS:

*(a) HEH: 5⅝ x 9¼ in.; pen and watercolor. There are several minor differences from the print, especially in the labels on the bottles. The mirror in the print that reflects the face of Death is a sign in the drawing. The printing on the sign is clipped: "GREA / allow / to / deale / in / Qual / Med."

(b) HCL: 5¾ x 9 9/16 in.; pen and watercolor; close to (a).

(c) Philip Hofer: 5 x 8 in.; pen and watercolor; signed "Rowlandson." Mounted with the drawing is a handwritten label with the title "The Quack Doctor" followed by the caption that appears on the print.

(d) Philip Hofer: in reverse; 4 15/16 x 7 15/16 in.; pen and watercolor; signed "Rowlandson"; started as a counterproof from (c).

The theme of Death and the doctor was popular with authors of Dances of Death. Rowlandson himself has more than one drawing involving the theme. For a discussion of this subject see Aldred Scott Warthin, *The Physician of the Dance of Death* (New York, 1931).

12. THE SOT

PRINT:

London, Pub. July 1, 1814 at R. Ackermann's, 101 Strand.

Drunk and alive, the man was thine,
But dead & drunk, why,—he is mine.

4 7/16 x 7¾ in.

First state: the figure seated with his back to the spectator has aquatint around only the edge of his back. The normal color scheme has the sot's coat blue and his waistcoat yellow.

DRAWINGS:

*(a) HEH: 5 11/16 x 9 5/16 in.; pen and watercolor; squared off in pencil; clear remnants of preparatory pencil work beneath the ink; closer to the print than (b).

(b) HEH: 5 11/16 x 9¼ in.; pen and watercolor; minor differences from (a); pencil inscription on verso that appears to be in Rowlandson's hand: "This is to be a drunken Exiseman instead of minding the kings interest gets drunk & lets the Country & Revenue be cheated."

The design is close (in reverse) to a print by Rowlandson issued on November 30, 1810: "Doctor Drainbarrel conveyed Home in a Wheelbarrow, in order to take his trial for Neglect of Family Duty." Combe's verses do not relate in any way to the pencil inscription on the verso of drawing (b).

13. THE HONEY MOON

PRINT:

London, Pub. Augt. 1, 1814 at R. Ackermann's, 101 Strand.

When the old fool has drank his wine
And gone to rest, I will be thine.

4 13/16 x 8 in.

Second state: there is a smudge on the young lover's nose. The normal color scheme has the sofa pink, the woman's dress yellow.

DRAWINGS:

*(a) HEH: 4¾ x 8⅛ in.; pen and watercolor; squared off in pencil.

(b) Ashmolean: 4 13/16 x 8 1/16 in.; pen and watercolor; inscribed "The Honey Moon" and signed "Rowlandson"; the writing is in Rowlandson's hand; probably began as a tracing from (a). On the old mount is a handwritten label entitled "The Honey Moon" followed by the caption that appears on the print. Also on the mount in pencil in a mid-nineteenth-century hand is the word "Copy." This drawing, together with three others in the Ashmolean for the Dance of Death, are said to be copies by Miss Howitt (see Introduction, pp. 19-25).

14. THE HUNTER UNKENNELLED

PRINT:

London, Pub. Augt. 1, 1814 at R. Ackermann's, 101 Strand.

Yes, Nimrod, you may look aghast:
I have unkennel'd you at last.

4 13/16 x 8 in.

First state: no aquatint behind Death's hand holding the tablecloth. The normal color scheme has the coats of the seated man and the man beneath the table in brown.

DRAWING:

* HEH: 5¾ x 9⅜ in.; pen and watercolor; inscribed "Nothing certain in this Life"; squared off in pencil; a slight pencil sketch on verso.

15. THE GOOD MAN, DEATH, AND THE DOCTOR

PRINT:

London, Pub. Augt. 1, 1814, at R. Ackermann's, 101 Strand.

No scene so blest in Virtue's eyes,
As when the Man of Virtue dies.

4⅞ x 8 3/16 in.

First state: no aquatint on the right arm of the doctor. The color schemes differ considerably, but the bed curtain is normally green, the kneeling woman's dress blue.

DRAWINGS:

(a) HEH: 4¾ x 8 1/16 in.; pen and watercolor. The following drawing is clearly a counterproof derived from this one. It is interesting, in this connection, that many flexible but rather coarse lines in sanguine were added to (a) after the counterproof was pulled.

(b) HEH: in reverse; 4¾ x 8 in.; pen and watercolor; counterproof derived from (a); not fully inked over or colored.

*(c) Ashmolean: 4 15/16 x 8¼ in.; pen and watercolor; signed "Rowlandson"; possibly began as

a tracing from (a). On the old mount is a handwritten label entitled "The Good Man, Death and the Doctor" followed by the same caption that appears on the print. Also on the old mount in pencil in a mid-nineteenth-century hand is the word "Copy." Said to be a copy by Miss Howitt (see Introduction, pp. 19-25).

(d) HCL: 4¼ x 5 11/16 in.; pen and wash; a free sketch with numerous variations from the published design.

16. DEATH AND THE PORTRAIT

PRINT:

London, Pub. Septr. 1, 1814, at R. Ackermann's, 101 Strand.

Nature and Truth are not at strife:
Death draws his pictures after Life.

4⅝ x 8⅛ in.

First state: no aquatint along the top edge of the palette. The normal color scheme has the screen blue, the old man's suit purple, and Death's chair red. There is a colored proof before aquatint in HCL.

DRAWINGS:

*(a) HEH: 5⅝ x 9¼ in.; pen, watercolor, and preliminary pencil (unfinished); inscribed "a Hasty Sketch or the Finishing Touch." There are numerous differences from the finished design, the most important being that Death has given the old man horns in the portrait and represents himself in the painting as kissing the old man's cheek.

(b) NYP: 4¾ x 8⅛ in.; pen and watercolor; much closer to the print than (a). The portrait on the easel is inscribed "Picture of Death" (not present in the print); the young man holds a drawing of an amorous couple (changed to a group of *putti* in the print).

The theme of infidelity, which was clearly Rowlandson's first thought, makes no appearance in the final design or in Combe's verses. Rowlandson had used a similar design (but without any reference to Death) in *Comforts of Bath* (London, 1798), Pl. 6.

17. THE GENEALOGIST

PRINT:

Pub. Septr. 1, 1814, at R. Ackermann's 101 Strand.

On that illumin'd roll of Fame
Death waits to write your Lordship's name.

4¾ x 8⅛ in.

First state: the wash of aquatint on the scroll has a jagged upper edge. The normal color scheme has the lady's skirt yellow and the man's coat red.

DRAWINGS:

* (a) HEH: in reverse; 4¾ x 8⅛ in.; pen and watercolor; the outlines of the figures have been carefully but lightly traced over by some sort of pencil that has left a silvery deposit visible in raking light. Although the drawing is the reverse of the print, there are none of the customary indications that the drawing began as a counterproof.

(b) Achenbach Foundation for Graphic Arts, California Palace of the Legion of Honor: 4¾ x 8½ in.; pen and watercolor (unfinished); the scroll held by Death is inscribed "Servant's / Office / Bond Street."

18. THE CATCHPOLE

PRINT:

Pub. Septr. 1, 1814, at R. Ackermann's, 101 Strand.

The Catchpole need not fear a jail,
The Undertaker is his Bail.

4 9/16 x 7⅞ in. (margin not square).

First state: no aquatint on Death's dart. The normal color scheme has the young man's coat blue, the catchpole's coat brown and his waistcoat rust. A colored proof before aquatint is in HCL.

DRAWING:

* HEH: 5⅝ x 9¼ in.; pen and watercolor; indications of preparatory pencil work beneath. There is a figure of a woman pumping water on the right which is not present in the print. Although the drawing is larger than the print, the scale of the figures included in both is actually the same. The sign above the door is inscribed: "Cathpole / Sherriffs Officer."

19. THE INSURANCE OFFICE

PRINT:

London, Pub. Octr. 1, 1814, at R. Ackermann's, 101 Strand.

Insure his Life.—But to your sorrow,
You'll pay a good, round Sum tomorrow.

4⅞ x 8⅛ in.

The Huntington impressions all appear to be of the same state. The normal color scheme has the customer's coat blue and his waistcoat pink.

DRAWINGS:

*(a) HEH: 5 11/16 x 9 5/16 in.; pen and watercolor, considerable reinforcement in sanguine; squared off in pencil, and also on the back (the lines on the back coinciding in position with those on front); numbered "87" on verso.

(b) NYP: 4 11/16 x 7⅞ in.; pen and watercolor.

(c) HEH: in reverse; 4 13/16 x 8 3/16 in.; pen and watercolor; signed "Rowlandson." Mounted with the drawing is a handwritten label entitled "The Insurance Office" followed by the caption that appears on the print. This drawing began as a counterproof almost certainly pulled from (b).

20. THE SCHOOLMASTER

PRINT:

London, Pub. Octr. 1, 1814, at R. Ackermanns, 101 Strand.

Death, with his dart proceeds to flog
Th'astonish'd, flogging Pedagogue.

4⅞ x 7 11/16 in.

First state: the hour hand on the clock is barely visible; the hands are re-etched in later states. The normal color scheme has the teacher's gown green and his cap red. There is a colored proof before aquatint in HCL.

DRAWING:

* HEH: 5 x 7 15/16 in.; pen and watercolor; the globes and books inscribed as in the print with minor exceptions; the group of children running out the door includes girls; in the print they are all boys.

A similar subject appears in J. R. Schellenberg, *Freund Heins Erscheinungen in Holbeins Manier* (Winterthur, 1785).

21. THE COQUETTE

PRINT:

London, Pub. Octr. 1, 1814, at R. Ackermann's, 101 Strand.

I'll lead you to the splendid Croud:
But your next dress will be a shroud.

4¾ x 8 in.

First state: there is a smudge of aquatint in the lower right corner of the mirror. The normal color scheme has the robe held by the maid pink and Death's coat rust.

DRAWINGS:

* (a) HEH: 5¾ x 9¼ in.; pen and watercolor; squared off in pencil; unfinished.

(b) HEH: 4⅞ x 8 3/16 in.; pen and watercolor; squared off in pencil, the positions of the lines corresponding to those in (a); signed "Rowlandson"; there is a handwritten label mounted with the drawing entitled "The Coquette" followed by the same caption as on the print.

A similar subject appears in J. R. Schellenberg, *Freund Heins Erscheinungen in Holbeins Manier* (Winterthur, 1785).

22. TIME & DEATH, AND GOODY BARTON

PRINT:

London, Pub. Novr. 1, 1814, at R. Ackermann's, 101 Strand.

On with your dead; & I'll contrive
To bury this old fool alive.

4⅞ x 8⅜ in.

Second state: spots of aquatint have been added to reinforce the lines of the rib cage in the extreme lower right corner. The normal color scheme has the hoisted man's coat blue and trousers rust.

DRAWINGS:

(a) HEH: 4⅞ x 8 7/16 in.; pen and watercolor; signed "Rowlandson"; there is a handwritten label mounted with the drawing entitled "Time & Death, and Goody Barton" followed by the same caption as on the print. This is a variant design with Death driving the cart and a young woman hoisting up Goody Barton; Time is not present.

(b) NYP: in reverse; 4¾ x 8⅜ in.; pen and watercolor; same variations from the print as in (a); began as a counterproof pulled from (a).

* (c) Paul Mellon: 5¼ x 8 7/16 in.; pen and watercolor; close to the print.

23. THE UNDERTAKER & THE QUACK

PRINT:

London, Pub. Novr. 1, 1814, at R. Ackermann's, 101 Strand.

The Doctor's sick'ning toil to close,
"Recipe Coffin," is the Dose.

4 13/16 x 8 5/16 in.

First state: no aquatint on the windowpanes behind the man on crutches. The normal color scheme has the quack's suit brown, the coat of the man on crutches blue. There is a colored proof before aquatint in HCL.

DRAWINGS:

*(a) HEH: 4 13/16 x 8 5/16 in.; pen and watercolor; sign to left: "Peter Screwtight / appraiser and / Undertaker / Funerals furnishd." Sign left background: "Real Home / Brewed / Bob Quashi." Sign to right: "Deadus Best / Cordial Gin." The last sign is changed on the print to read "Old Ram / Inn."

(b) HEH: in reverse; 4¾ x 8¼ in.; pen and watercolor; signed "Rowlandson." There is a handwritten label mounted with the drawing entitled "The Undertaker & the Quack" followed by the caption that appears on the print. This drawing began as a counterproof pulled from (a); the signs are in reverse except for the "Deadus Best" sign, which does not appear and must have been added to (a) after the counterproof was pulled.

(c) NYP: 4¾ x 8 1/16 in.; pen and watercolor; the "Peter Screwtight" sign is as in (a); the other signs are absent. There are numerous minor variations from (a), which is closer to the print.

The figure of the quack is so similar to that of the quack doctor in No. 11 that Rowlandson may have intended a connection.

24. THE MASQUERADE

*PRINT:

London, Pub. Novr. 1, 1814, at R. Ackermann's, 101 Strand.

Such is the power, & such the strife,
That ends the Masquerade of Life.

4¾ x 8 1/16 in.

Second state: the aquatint wash covers all of the back wall. The normal color scheme has Death's cloak blue.

DRAWINGS:

No drawings for this subject have been located. The same theme, in an unrelated design, occurs in an unpublished drawing (No. 79). A similar subject occurs in Salomon Van Rusting, *Schau-Platz des Todes, oder Todten-Tanz* (Nuremberg, 1736).

25. THE DEATH BLOW

PRINT:

London, Pub. Decr. 1, 1814, at R. Ackermann's, 101 Strand.

How vain are all your triumphs past,
For this Set-To will be your last.

4 7/16 x 8⅜ in.

First state: the aquatint cloud behind the trees to the right is very faint. The normal color scheme has the standing boxer's trousers brown, the fallen boxer's trousers pink.

DRAWING:

* HEH: in reverse; 4 7/16 x 7 13/16 in.; pen and watercolor; inscribed "A Rum Customer." There are traces of preliminary pencil work beneath the pen lines, suggesting that (although the drawing is the reverse of the print) it did not begin as a counterproof.

There is another Rowlandson drawing in the Huntington collection involving a boxing match with Death, but the style and format of the drawing imply that it is not directly connected with the *English Dance of Death* series.

26. THE VISION OF SKULLS

PRINT:

London, Pub. Decr. 1, 1814, at R. Ackermann's, 101 Strand.

As it appears, though dead so long,
Each scull is found to have a tongue.

4¾ x 8¼ in.

First state: the edges of the arches in the background are not defined by etched lines. The normal color scheme has the fat woman in a white dress with yellow mantle; the fat man in a blue coat and pink waistcoat. There is a colored proof before aquatint in HCL.

DRAWINGS:

*(a) HEH: 4 13/16 x 8⅝ in.; pen and watercolor, with preparatory pencil.

(b) NYP: in reverse; 4¾ x 8 in.; pen and watercolor; started as a counterproof pulled from (a) but has been reinforced throughout.

(c) John Rickett: 5 x 8⅝ in.; pen and watercolor; signed "Rowlandson"; several minor variations from (a) and (b) and from the print.

The version of this drawing in the possession of Mr. Rickett bears an apparently contemporary inscription (not in Rowlandson's hand) supplying "English in Paris" as an alternative title. The suggestion is certainly a plausible one. There do not appear to have been any catacombs or ossuaries in England of the type Rowlandson illustrates. Moreover, the Paris catacombs at "la Tombe-Issoire" were attracting attention at the time. They had been established in the 1780's in old Roman quarries when several Paris cemeteries, notably that of the Innocents, were closed. A book by L. Héricart de Thury, *Descriptions des catacombes de Paris*, was published in 1815.

Rowlandson was in Paris on more than one occasion and may have been among the scores of English travelers who took advantage of the lull in the Napoleonic wars while Napoleon was in exile on Elba (April 1814 until February 1815) to visit the French capital.

DRAWINGS:

*(a) HEH: 5¼ x 8¾ in.; pen and watercolor, with preparatory pencil; inscribed "The Warning or Death's Watch."

(b) NYP: in reverse; 5 x 8⅛ in. (uneven); pen and watercolor; signed "Rowlandson 1806"; started as a counterproof pulled from (a). The inscription appears to be in Rowlandson's hand, but the date must be in error. This would not be the only instance known in which Rowlandson appears to have misdated his own drawings.

27. THE PORTER'S CHAIR

PRINT:

London, Pub. Decr. 1, 1814, at R. Ackermann's, 101 Strand.

What watchful Care the Portal keeps!
A Porter He, who never sleeps.

4¾ x 8⅜ in.

First state: no aquatint on the section of wall adjacent to the right side of Death's chair. The normal color scheme has Death's chair red, the shirt of the man with a sword yellow.

28. THE PANTOMIME

PRINT:

London Pub. Jany. 1, 1815, at R. Ackermann's, 101 Strand.

Behold the signal of Old Time:
That bids you close your Pantomime.

4¾ x 8⅛ in.

Second state: the etched lines on the bank above and to the left of the principal group are obscured by aquatint. The normal color scheme has Pantaloon in yellow with red stripes, Pierrot in white, Harlequin in motley blue, pink, and yellow.

DRAWINGS:

*(a) HEH: 5⅝ x 9⅛ in.; pen and watercolor. The figures of Pantaloon and Pierrot are considerably reinforced in sanguine.

(b) HEH: 4¾ x 8¼ in.; pen and watercolor.

(c) NYP: in reverse; 4¾ x 8⅛ in.; pen and watercolor; started as a counterproof pulled from (b).

29. THE HORSE RACE

PRINT:

London, Pub. Jany. 1, 1815, at R. Ackermann's, 101 Strand.

This is a very break Neck Heat;
And Squire Jockey you are beat.

4⅞ x 8½ in.

Second state: the etched lines have been extensively reinforced, noticeably in the broken line around the top of the "Betting Post" sign. The normal color scheme has the rider's coat blue and trousers yellow.

DRAWING:

* HEH: 5⅛ x 8½ in.; pen and watercolor, with preparatory pencil; a free sketch, but close to the print.

30. THE DRAM SHOP

PRINT:

London, Pub. Jany. 1, 1815, at R. Ackermann's, 101 Strand.

Some find their Death by Sword & Bullet;
And some by fluids down the Gullet.

5 x 8¼ in.

Second state: the outlines of the figure smoking a pipe have been broadened with aquatint. The normal color scheme has the woman of the amorous seated couple in yellow, the man's trousers blue and his coat pink. There is a colored proof before aquatint in HCL.

DRAWING:

* HEH: in reverse; 5¼ x 8⅝ in.; pen and watercolor; preparatory pencil work; inscribed in pencil "Gin Shop" and another undecipherable word (possibly "Rumbarels"). The labels on the barrels are not precisely the same as in the print: the largest is "Old Tom," the next is "77," the pitcher on "Old Tom" is labeled "Vitriol." The drawing does not seem to have started as a counterproof, although the appearance of some lines suggests that a counterproof was pulled from it.

31. THE GAMING TABLE

PRINT:

London, Pub. Feby. 1, 1815, at R. Ackermann's, 101 Strand.

Whene'er Death plays, He's sure to win:
He'll take each knowing Gamester in.

5 x 8 7/16 in.

First state: the curtain to the left has a uniform wash of aquatint.

DRAWING:

* HEH: in reverse; 5¼ x 8⅝ in.; pen and watercolor, with preparatory pencil. The pencil work indicates that although the drawing is the reverse of the print, it probably did not start as a counterproof. The appearance of the lines, however, strongly suggests that a counterproof was pulled from the drawing.

The subject of gambling is a favorite one in the various Dances of Death. Holbein used it in both the alphabet series and the great Dance of Death.

32. THE BATTLE

PRINT:

London, Pub. 1 Feby. 1815, at R. Ackermann's 101 Strand.

Such is, alas, the common Story
Of Blood & Wounds, of Death & Glory.

5 x 8½ in.

Second state: the group firing the cannon has been reinforced with additional etching lines and aquatint; the sword of the officer becomes a continuous line; the ramrod behind him is reinforced with aquatint. The normal color scheme has the coats red and the saddle cloths blue.

DRAWING:

* HEH: 5 1/16 x 8 7/16 in.; pen and watercolor; a free sketch with several minor variations from the print.

At the time this print was issued Napoleon was still in exile on Elba, and no major military campaign was in progress. Napoleon escaped from Elba on February 26, 1815.

33. THE WEDDING

PRINT:

London, Pub. Feby. 1, 1815, at R. Ackermann's, 101 Strand.

Plutus commands, & to the Arms
Of doting Age, She yeilds [sic] *her Charms.*

4⅞ x 8⅜ in.

Second state: several intense touches of aquatint on the base of the column to the left. The normal color scheme has the groom's suit purple, and that of the man behind him green.

* There is a colored proof before aquatint in HCL.

DRAWINGS:

No drawings have been located for this subject.

The theme of youth and age in marriage seems to have had particular interest for Rowlandson. It occurs in variation four times in the published designs for the *English Dance of Death.* The theme also appears in J. R. Schellenberg, *Freund Heins Erscheinungen in Holbeins Manier* (Winterthur, 1785).

34. THE SKAITERS

PRINT:

London, Pub. March 1. 1815, at R. Ackermann's, 101 Strand.

On the frail Ice, the whirring Skate
Becomes an Instrument of Fate

4¾ x 8⅛ in.

There does not appear to be a clear distinction in states among the four impressions in the Huntington Library. The normal color scheme has the girl falling backwards in the foreground in pink, the fat man about to fall on top of her in brown.

DRAWINGS:

*(a) HEH: 4¾ x 8 3/16 in.; pen and watercolor; signed "Rowlandson"; a rapid sketch with several minor variations from the print.

(b) NYP: 4⅝ x 8 in. (uneven trim); pen and watercolor with preparatory pencil; closer to the print than (a).

(c) HEH: in reverse; 4¾ x 8 in.; pen and watercolor; there is a handwritten label mounted with the drawing entitled "The Skaiters" followed by the caption that appears on the print. Began as a counterproof pulled from (b) but has been fully worked over.

The same subject occurs in Van Rusting, *Schau-Platz des Todes, oder Todten-Tanz* (Nuremberg, 1736).

35. THE DUEL

PRINT:

Pubd. March 1. 1815, at R. Ackermann's, 101 Strand.

Here Honour, as it is the mode,
To Death consigns the weighty load.

4 15/16 x 8⅜ in.

First state: no aquatint on the light area of the bank behind Death. The normal color scheme has the coat of the falling man blue, his breeches brown, the coat of the man on the extreme right green.

DRAWING:

* HEH: 4 13/16 x 8 7/16 in.; pen and watercolor; traces of preliminary pencil work. The appearance of many of the lines indicates that a counterproof was probably pulled from the drawing, but the pencil work implies that the drawing did not itself begin as a counterproof.

Dueling was still prevalent in Rowlandson's day, but the law was beginning to take a firmer view of the matter. A notable case arose in 1813, when, following the death of a Lieutenant Blundell in a duel, the surviving principal and the seconds were all convicted of murder and sentenced to death. A royal pardon was obtained, but all the men were cashiered.

36. THE BISHOP AND DEATH

PRINT:

London, Pub. March 1, 1815, at R. Ackermann's, 101 Strand.

Though I may yield my forfeit breath,
The word of Life defies thee, Death.

4⅞ x 8 5/16 in.

First state: no aquatint on the window panes. The normal color scheme has the chair upholstery pink, the floor green. There is a colored proof before aquatint in HCL.

DRAWINGS:

*(a) HEH: 5¼ x 8 3/16 in.; pen and watercolor, with preliminary pencil; signed "Rowlandson"; mounted with the drawing is a handwritten label entitled "The Bishop and Death" followed by the same caption that appears on the print.

(b) NYP: in reverse; 4¾ x 8 1/16 in.; pen and watercolor; began as a counterproof, but not clearly derived from (a).

(c) Sotheby's, November 20, 1928, Lot 70: 5¾ x 9¼ in.; present whereabouts unknown.

The theme of the bishop and Death is a traditional subject for the Dance of Death.

37. THE SUICIDE

PRINT:

London, Pub. April 1, 1815, at R. Ackermann's, 101 Strand.

Death smiles & seems his dart to hide;
When He beholds the Suicide.

4 11/16 x 7 15/16 in.

Second state: the etched lines of the foam on the waves breaking beneath the woman have been reinforced with aquatint. The normal color scheme has the woman's dress white and her shawl pink.

DRAWINGS:

*(a) HEH: in reverse; 5⅝ x 9 3/16 in.; pen and watercolor with remnants of preparatory pencil; inscribed: "She died for love and he for glory." Although the drawing is the reverse of the print, there is no indication that it began as a counterproof or that a counterproof was pulled from it. Aside from the reversal, the principal difference from the print is in the position of the floating body.

(b) NYP: in reverse; 4 9/16 x 7 13/16 in.; pen and watercolor; some of the lines suggest that a counterproof may have been pulled; closer to the print than (a).

38. CHAMPAGNE, SHERRY, AND WATER GRUEL

PRINT:

London, Pub. April 1, 1815, at R. Ackermann's, 101 Strand.

Have patience Death, nor be so cruel
To spoil the Sick man's Watergruel.

4⅝ x 7 13/16 in.

All impressions in the Huntington Library appear to be of the same state. The normal color scheme has the man taking gruel in pink, the fat man in blue coat with yellow waistcoat.

DRAWINGS:

*(a) HEH: 5 3/16 x 8½ in.; pen and watercolor with preparatory pencil; inscribed, from left to right, "The Bon Vivant—The Moderate Man—The Abstemious Man."

(b) HEH: 4 11/16 x 7⅞ in.; pen and watercolor with preparatory pencil; closer to the print than (a).

(c) NYP: in reverse; 4 7/16 x 7 11/16 in.; pen and watercolor; possibly began as a counterproof pulled from (b), but reinforced throughout.

39. THE NURSERY

PRINT:

London, Pub. April 1, 1815, at R. Ackermann's, 101 Strand.

Death rocks the cradle: Life is o'er:
The Infant sleeps, to wake no more.

4⅞ x 8⅛ in.

First state: no hands visible on the face of the clock. The normal color scheme has the mother's dress white, her blouse and bonnet yellow, her cape pink.

DRAWINGS:

(a) HCL: in reverse; 5 13/16 x 9⅜ in.; pen and watercolor with preparatory pencil; several variations from the print, the most important being that the child is obviously not yet dead. There is no evidence that this drawing began as a counterproof.

(b) HEH: in reverse; 4⅞ x 8⅛ in.; pen and watercolor with some preparatory pencil; closer to the print than (a). There is no evidence that this drawing began as a counterproof.

*(c) Dr. Morris H. Saffron: 4¾ x 8 in.; pen and watercolor; signed "Rowlandson"; there is a handwritten label mounted with the drawing entitled "The Nursery" followed by the caption that appears on the print.

The theme of Death in the nursery is a common one in the Dance of Death. It is present in both Holbein's treatments of the theme; also in J. R. Schellenberg, *Freund Heins Erscheinungen in Holbeins Manier* (Winterthur, 1785).

40. THE ASTRONOMER

PRINT:

London, Pub. May 1, 1815, at R. Ackermann's, 101 Strand.

Why I was looking at the Bear:
But what strange Planet see I there!

4 13/16 x 8¼ in.

First state: the bust on the cabinet to the left has a highlight only along the profile. The normal color scheme has the astronomer's robe green and the chair pink. There is a colored proof before aquatint in HCL.

DRAWINGS:

*(a) HCL: 5 11/16 x 8¾ in.; pen and watercolor with preparatory pencil; numerous variations from the print, the most important being the introduction of an abduction scene in the background, where the startled woman stands in the print. Death kneels on a chart inscribed "Variations of Moon."

(b) HEH: 5 x 8⅜ in.; pen and watercolor; signed "Rowlandson"; there is a handwritten label mounted with the drawing entitled "The Astronomer" followed by the caption that appears on the print; closer to the print than (a) but still with minor variations. A chart on the wall is inscribed "Planisphere."

41. THE FATHER OF THE FAMILY

PRINT:

London, Pub. May 1, 1815, at R. Ackermann's, 101 Strand.

The Doctors say that you're my booty:
Come Sir, for I must do my duty.

4 15/16 x 8¼ in.

The impressions in the Huntington Library all appear to be of the same state. The normal color scheme has the young father's coat green, the dress of the woman immediately behind him pink.

DRAWING:

* HEH: 5¾ x 9 5/16 in.; pen and watercolor; squared off in pencil; inscribed verso in pencil, "taken in the prime of life."

42. THE FALL OF FOUR IN HAND

PRINT:

London, Pub. May 1, 1815, at R. Ackermann's, 101 Strand.

Death can contrive to strike his blows
By overturns and overthrows.

4¾ x 8 1/16 in.

All the impressions in the Huntington Library appear to be of the same state. The normal color scheme has the horses brown, the coat of the rider to the right green. A colored proof before aquatint is in HCL.

DRAWINGS:

*(a) HEH: 5 x 8½ in.; pen and watercolor with preparatory pencil.

(b) NYP: in reverse; 4½ x 8 in.; pen and watercolor; began as a counterproof, probably pulled from (a).

43. GAFFER GOODMAN

PRINT:

Pub. June 1, 1815, at R. Ackermann's, 101 Strand.

Another Whiff and all is o'er,
And Gaffer Goodman is no more.

4½ x 7⅜ in.

The impressions in the Huntington Library all appear to be of the same state. The normal color scheme has Gaffer Goodman's gown purple, his cap green.

DRAWINGS:

(a) NYP: 4 3/16 x 6 15/16 in.; pen and watercolor; unfinished.

*(b) HEH: in reverse; 4 7/16 x 7 3/16 in.; pen and watercolor; clearly began as a counterproof pulled from (a) but has been worked out much further than (a).

44. THE URCHIN ROBBERS

PRINT:

Pub. June 1, 1815, at R. Ackermann's, 101 Strand.
O the unconscionable Brute!
To murder for a little Fruit!
4¾ x 8 in.

Second state: the bricks of the chimney to the left are outlined in aquatint. The normal color scheme has the man's coat red, the pump blue.

DRAWING:

* HEH: in reverse; 4¾ x 8 in.; pen and watercolor; although the composition is the reverse of the print, there are no indications that the drawing began as a counterproof or that a counterproof was pulled from it.

45. DEATH TURNED PILOT

PRINT:

Pub. June 1, 1815, at R. Ackermann's, 101 Strand.
The fatal Pilot grasps the Helm,
And steers the Crew to Pluto's Realm.
4 9/16 x 7 15/16 in.

Second state: the bowsprit of the sinking ship to the right is reinforced with aquatint. The normal color scheme has the dress of the woman pink, the jackets of the men blue.

DRAWINGS:

*(a) HEH: 5¾ x 9 5/16 in.; pen and watercolor; squared off in pencil.

(b) NYP: 5⅜ x 9⅛ in. (uneven trim); pen and watercolor.

(c) Paul Mellon: 5⅞ x 9⅜ in.; pen and watercolor.

(d) Formerly with Fitz Eugene Dixon of Philadelphia; present whereabouts unknown: 5½ x 9¼ in. American Art Association, January 6 and 7, 1937, Lot 139.

A ship in distress is a subject used by Holbein in his large Dance of Death. The theme of the lifeboat following shipwreck was treated earlier by Rowlandson in a print probably issued in 1799 (see Grego, *Rowlandson the Caricaturist* [London, 1880], I, 372-374).

46. THE WINDING UP OF THE CLOCK

PRINT:

London, Pub. July 1, 1815, at R. Ackermann's, 101 Strand.

"No one but me shall set my Clock."
He set it & behold the Shock.

4¾ x 8 1/16 in.

First state: no aquatint on the window panes. The normal color scheme has the chair and curtains pink, the floor green.

DRAWINGS:

* (a) HEH: 4 13/16 x 8 3/16 in.; pen and watercolor.
(b) NYP: in reverse; 4⅝ x 7⅞ in.; pen and watercolor; began as a counterproof pulled from (a).

47. THE FAMILY OF CHILDREN

PRINT:

London, Pub. July 1, 1815, at R. Ackermann's, 101 Strand.

'Twere well to spare me two or three
Out of your num'rous Family.

4 13/16 x 8¼ in.

Second state: the etched lines of the window mullions are covered by an aquatint wash. The normal color scheme has the window curtains and bench pink, the man's coat blue. There is a colored proof before aquatint in HCL.

DRAWINGS:

* (a) HEH: 4⅞ x 8⅛ in.; pen and watercolor.
(b) Paul Mellon: 4⅜ x 7⅜ in.; pen and watercolor.

48. DEATH'S DOOR

PRINT:

London, Pub. July 1, 1815, at R. Ackermann's, 101 Strand.

In this world all our Comfort's o'er;
So let us find it at Death's Door.

4¾ x 8 in.

First state: no aquatint on the foreground in front of the crutches. The normal color scheme has the fat woman's gown pink with blue underskirt, the man knocking in green and yellow.

DRAWINGS:

* (a) HEH: in reverse; 6 x 9½ in.; pen and watercolor; there are many variations from the print, aside from the reversal. This drawing clearly began

as a counterproof, which has then been extensively reinforced, but the drawing from which the proof was pulled is not now known.

(b) HEH: 4¾ x 8⅛ in.; pen and watercolor with remnants of preliminary pencil; signed "Rowlandson"; mounted with the drawing is a handwritten label with the title "Death's Door" followed by the caption that appears on the print; much closer to the print than (a).

(c) NYP: in reverse; 4 11/16 x 8 in. (uneven trim); pen and watercolor; although the drawing clearly began as a counterproof, it does not appear to have been pulled from (b).

49. THE FIRE

PRINT:

London, Pub. Augt. 1, 1815, at R. Ackermann's, 101 Strand.

Let him go on with all his rigs;
We're safe. He'll only burn the pigs.

5 1/16 x 8½ in.

Second state: an aquatint shadow has been added along the left leg and foot of Death. The normal color scheme has the clouds of smoke pink. There is a colored proof before aquatint in HCL.

DRAWINGS:

*(a) Philip Hofer: 5¼ x 8 7/16 in.; pen and watercolor; signed "Rowlandson"; close to the print except for the upraised fist of the man carrying the bucket and the position of Death's head; mounted with the drawing is a handwritten label entitled "The Fire" followed by the caption that appears on the print.

(b) NYP: in reverse; 4¾ x 8¼ in.; pen and watercolor; clearly began as a counterproof, probably pulled from (a).

50. THE MISER'S END

PRINT:

London, Pub. Augt. 1, 1815, at R. Ackermann's, 101 Strand.

Old Dad, at length, is grown so kind;
He dies, & leaves his wealth behind.

4 15/16 x 8⅛ in.

Second state: an aquatint shadow has been added across the bottom halves of the two money bags in the left foreground. The normal color scheme has the miser's blanket purple, the heir's coat blue.

DRAWING:

* HEH: 5 13/16 x 9⅜ in.; pen and watercolor; squared off in pencil; some variations from the print, especially in the figure to the right above the miser. The chart on the wall is inscribed, "Mortgages / Leases / expiring / Life Annuities / Scrip / Omnium / Loans / Bank Stock / South Sea"; the bust is labeled "Midas"; the book beneath the miser's left hand, "Book of Interest."

The theme of Death and the miser was a normal one for the Dance of Death; it occurs in both Holbein series and in J. R. Schellenberg, *Freund Heins Erscheinungen in Holbeins Manier* (Winterthur, 1785).

51. GRETNA GREEN

PRINT:

London, Pub. Augt. 1, 1815 at R. Ackermann's, 101 Strand.

Love, spread your wings; I'll not outstrip 'em:
Though Death's behind, He will not clip 'em.

4 13/16 x 8⅛ in.

Second state: the tire of the rear left wheel of the carriage has an aquatint wash from top to bottom. The normal color scheme has the coats of the postilions blue, the coat of the pursuing horseman purple.

DRAWINGS:

*(a) HEH: 4 13/16 x 8 in.; pen and watercolor.

(b) NYP: in reverse; 4 13/16 x 8 in. (uneven trim); pen and watercolor; started as a counterproof pulled from (a).

Gretna Green, just over the Scottish border, became the popular resort of eloping couples after 1754, when an act abolishing clandestine marriages in England came into force. The traffic died down after 1856 when a law was passed requiring one of the contracting parties to be resident in Scotland for at least three weeks prior to the event.

52. THE WALTZ

PRINT:

Pub. Septr. 1, 1815, at R. Ackermann's, 101 Strand.

By Gar, that horrid, strange Buffoon
Cannot keep time to any tune.

4¾ x 7 11/16 in.

The impressions in the Huntington Library appear to be of one state. The normal color scheme has Death's cloak purple; the dancing master's coat red, waistcoat green, and breeches blue.

DRAWINGS:

*(a) HEH: 4 13/16 x 7⅞ in.; pen and watercolor with preparatory pencil.

(b) HEH: in reverse; 4 11/16 x 7¾ in.; pen and watercolor; signed "Rowlandson"; mounted with the drawing is a handwritten label entitled "The Waltz" followed by the same caption as on the print; started as a counterproof pulled from (a).

53. MATERNAL TENDERNESS

*PRINT:

Pub. Septr. 1, 1815, at R. Ackermanns, 101 Strand.

Thus it appears a pond of Water
May prove an Instrument of Slaughter.

4¾ x 8⅛ in.

The impressions in the Huntington Library all appear to be of the same state. The normal color scheme has the swooning lady in pink, the man beside her in brown.

DRAWINGS:

No drawings for this subject have been located.

54. THE KITCHEN

PRINT:

London, Pub. Septr. 1, 1815, at R. Ackermann's, 101 Strand.

Thou Slave to ev'ry gorging Glutton,
I'll spit thee like a Leg of Mutton.

4 13/16 x 8¼ in.

The impressions in the Huntington Library all appear to be of one state. The normal color scheme has the prostrate woman in green with a blue apron, the cook in a pink shirt.

DRAWINGS:

*(a) HEH: 5¼ x 8¾ in.; pen and watercolor.

(b) HEH: in reverse; 4¾ x 8¼ in.; pen and watercolor; began as a counterproof pulled from (a), extensively reworked and trimmed.

55. THE GIG

PRINT:

London, Pub. Octr. 1, 1815, at R. Ackermann's, 101 Strand.

Away they go in chaise & one,
Or to undo or be undone.

4¾ x 7 15/16 in.

First state: no aquatint on the front of the milestone. The normal color scheme has the lady in white, the man in a blue coat and brown breeches.

DRAWING:

* HEH: 4 15/16 x 8 3/16 in.; pen and watercolor with preparatory pencil.

56. THE MAUSOLEUM

PRINT:

London, Pub. Octr. 1, 1815, at R. Ackermann's, 101 Strand.

Your crabbed Dad is just gone home:
And now we look for joys to come.

4¾ x 8⅛ in.

Second state: the coachman is given an aquatint wash. The normal color scheme has the old man's gown green, the young man's coat red.

DRAWINGS:

*(a) Paul Mellon: 5 x 8¾ in.; pen and watercolor; signed "Rowlandson"; door inscribed "Mausoleum."

(b) HEH: in reverse; 4 13/16 x 8¼ in.; pen and watercolor (unfinished); clearly started as a counterproof (the word "mausoleum" on the door is backwards) pulled from (a).

57. THE COURTSHIP

PRINT:

London, Pub. Octr. 1, 1815, at R. Ackermann's, 101 Strand.

It is in vain that you decide:
Death claims you as his destin'd Bride.

4 13/16 x 8⅛ in.

All the impressions in the Huntington Library appear to be of the same state. The normal color scheme has the lady in white, all the chairs green, the man seated behind her in brown. There is a colored proof before aquatint in HCL.

DRAWINGS:

*(a) HEH: 5 11/16 x 9¼ in.; pen and watercolor; inscribed "A Tottering state, or a Man betwixts Life and Death." Inscribed verso: "Awkward state betwixt Life and Death" and "wants Explanation" and "this to go"; there is also a slight, undecipherable pencil sketch on the verso. Many minor variations from the print.

(b) NYP: in reverse; 4⅝ x 7¾ in. (uneven); pen and watercolor; began as a counterproof, but not pulled from (a).

58. THE TOASTMASTER

PRINT:

Pub. Novr. 1, 1815, at R. Ackermann's, 101 Strand.
The End of Life, the Chairman cries:
'Tis drank, & many a Toper dies.
4⅞ x 8 3/16 in.

Second state: an aquatint wash is added to the floor. The normal color scheme has the man whose glass is being filled in a purple coat and pink cap, the man who has fallen behind Death's chair in a blue coat. Philip Hofer has a colored proof before aquatint.

DRAWING:

* HEH: 5⅝ x 9 3/16 in.; pen and watercolor; signed and dated "Rowlandson 1805"; inscribed "Sots Hole"; several variations from the print, the most important being that the man behind the punch bowl spews into it. The date may be correct; the drawing appears to be somewhat earlier on the basis of style than others in the series.

The subject of a drunken debauch is frequent in treatments of the Dance of Death; Holbein uses it in his large series.

59. THE CARELESS AND THE CAREFUL

*PRINT:

London, Pub. Novr. 1, 1815, at R. Ackermann's, 101 Strand.
The Careful and the Careless led
To join the living and the dead.
4 11/16 x 8 7/16 in.

Second state: many lines of aquatint reinforcement have been added, especially noticeable on the edge of the skirt of the woman emerging from the archway. The normal color scheme has the ladies in white with a pink scarf to the left and a yellow to the right; Death's cloak is blue.

DRAWINGS:

No drawings for this subject have been located.

60. THE LAW OVERTHROWN

PRINT:

Pub. Novr. 1, 1815. R. Ackermann's, 101 Strand.

The Serjeant's tongue will cease to brawl
In every Court of yonder Hall.
4¾ x 8 7/16 in.

The impressions in the Huntington Library all appear to be of the same state. The normal color scheme has Death's cloak in blue, the cover of the driver's seat in pink.

DRAWINGS:

*(a) Dr. Morris Saffron: 5¼ x 8⅞ in.; pen and monochrome wash with preparatory pencil work; unfinished; mounted with the drawing is a handwritten label with the caption that appears on the print.

(b) HEH: in reverse; 4⅞ x 8⅝ in.; pen and watercolor with preparatory pencil work in the background; the principal group clearly began as a counterproof, probably pulled from (a).

The building in the background appears to be the entrance front of Westminster Hall.

61. THE FORTUNE TELLER

PRINT:

Pub. Decr. 1, 1815, at R. Ackermann's, 101 Strand.

All Fates he vow'd to him were known,
And yet He could not tell his own.
4¾ x 8¼ in.

All the impressions in the Huntington Library appear to be of the same state. The normal color scheme has the fortune teller in purple with a blue sash, his chair and table in green.

DRAWINGS:

*(a) HEH: 5 x 8 9/16 in.; pen and watercolor with preparatory pencil; unfinished.

(b) Ashmolean: in reverse; 5 x 8½ in. (uneven trim); pen and watercolor; started as a counterproof pulled from (a); further work was done on (a) after the counterproof was pulled. On the old mount of (b) is a handwritten label with the title "The Fortune Teller" followed by the caption that appears on the print. On the mount in pencil in a mid-nineteenth-century hand is the inscription "Copy by Miss Howitt" (see Introduction, pp. 19-25).

62. THE LOTTERY OFFICE

*PRINT:

Pub. Decr. 1, 1815, at R. Ackermann's, 101 Strand.

To trust to Fortune's smiles alone,
Is the High Road to be undone.
4 13/16 x 8 in.

In late impressions the numbers on the tickets held by Death become illegible, but the words "Doomesday Book" are made stronger. The normal color scheme has the lady in white with a pink bonnet, the man supporting her in a brown suit. There is a colored proof before aquatint in HCL.

DRAWING:

Sotheby, November 20, 1928: 4⅞ x 8¼ in.; wash; present whereabouts unknown.

Most private lotteries were prohibited in England, but government-sponsored lotteries continued to be a principal source of revenue. The annual government profit between 1793 and 1824 averaged just under £350,000. Lotteries were finally abolished in 1826.

63. THE PRISONER DISCHARGED

PRINT:

Pub. Decr. 1, 1815, at R. Ackermann's, 101 Strand.
Death, without either Bribe or Fee,
Can set the hopeless Pris'ner free.
4¾ x 8⅜ in.

First state: no aquatint in the center immediate foreground. The normal color scheme has the creditor's coat purple, the prisoner's coat blue.

DRAWING:

* HEH: 4¾ x 8 5/16 in.; pen and watercolor with preparatory pencil work; signed "Rowlandson"; the paper held by the creditor is inscribed "Bond / Judgm / Execut"; mounted with the drawing is a handwritten label entitled "The Prisoner Discharged" followed by the caption that appears on the print; the appearance of the ink lines on the drawing suggests that a counterproof was pulled from it.

As Combe points out in the verses accompanying the design, legislation introduced by Lord Redesdale in 1813 and 1814 had done a great deal for the relief of insolvent debtors. The hopeless plight of debtors implied by Rowlandson's design did not in fact exist at the time the print was issued.

64. THE GALLANT'S DOWNFALL

PRINT:

Pub. Jany. 1, 1816, at R. Ackermann's, 101 Strand.
The Assailant does not feel a wound:
But yet he dies, for he is drown'd.
4⅞ x 8 5/16 in.

Second state: etched lines are added to represent the gunfire. The normal color scheme has the young man's coat rust, the old man's coat blue.

DRAWING:

* HEH: 5 7/16 x 8¾ in.; pen and watercolor with preparatory pencil; a free drawing with several variations from the print, especially in the background; verso: a slight pencil sketch with figures outside a building.

65. THE CHURCH YARD DEBATE

PRINT:

Pubd. Jany. 1, 1816, at R. Ackermann's, 101 Strand.
Tis strange but true, in this world's Strife,
That Death affords the means of life.
4 13/16 x 8¼ in.

In the proof plate before aquatint the cleric holds the jug; in the impressions with aquatint it is on the ground. All impressions with aquatint in the Huntington Library appear to be of the same state. The normal color scheme has the lawyer's coat blue and the man smoking in purple.

DRAWINGS:

*(a) HEH: 5⅝ x 9 5/16 in.; pen and watercolor with preparatory pencil; the lawyer holds a paper inscribed "Last Will and Testament"; the sarcophagus to the right is inscribed "We live by Death"; on the wall an inscription, "Die All"; the man in the print who rings the bell is omitted; the cleric holds the jug as in the proof before aquatint.

(b) NYP: 4 13/16 x 8⅜ in.; pen and watercolor; closer to the print than (a), but the cleric still holds the jug.

A similar subject occurs in Newton's Dances of Death (London, 1796).

66. THE GOOD AND GREAT

*PRINT:

Pub. Jany. 1, 1816, at R. Ackermann's, 101 Strand.
What heart-felt Tears bedew the Dust
Of Him whose ev'ry thought was just.
5 x 8 1/16 in.

All impressions in the Huntington Library appear to be of the same state. The normal color scheme has the four figures in the lower right foreground in blue, purple, rust, and green (reading from left to right).

DRAWINGS:

There are no drawings known for this subject,

but an intimately related drawing is in the collection of Philip Hofer. In this drawing the background is close to the print, but the figure groups are entirely different. The subject is a funeral, but the figure of Death does not appear. The drawing is inscribed "Hatfield House Lord Salisburys"; 6 x 9½ in.; pen and watercolor. The inscription is puzzling if it is taken to refer to the funeral of a Lord Salisbury. James, 6th Earl of Salisbury, died in 1780, too early to have any direct connection with this drawing. His son James, 7th Earl and 1st Marquis of Salisbury, did not die until June 13, 1823. The background buildings do not appear to have any direct connection with Hatfield House.

67. THE NEXT HEIR

PRINT:

Pub. Feby. 1, 1816, at R. Ackermann's, 101 Strand.
'Tis not the time to meet one's fate,
Just ent'ring on a large Estate.
5 x 8 11/16 in.

Second state: the shadows in the dress of the lady in the carriage are strengthened with etched lines. The normal color scheme has the carriage yellow and the parasol green; the heir and his wife in black. A colored proof before aquatint is in HCL.

DRAWING:

* HEH: 5 x 8 15/16 in.; pen and monochrome gray wash with preparatory pencil; inscribed "Rowlandson" (not a signature). The background in the design is the same as in No. 66, "The Good and Great."

The theme of Death and the newly married couple occurs in Holbein.

68. THE CHAMBER WAR

PRINT:

Pub. Feby. 1, 1816, at R. Ackermann's, 101 Strand.
When Doctors three the Labour share,
No wonder Death attends them there.
4 11/16 x 8¼ in.

Second state: the whole plate is to a great extent re-etched; a second label is added to the neck of the bottle in the foreground. The normal color scheme has the sick man in a green coat and purple breeches; the doctor nearest him in a purple suit and pink waistcoat.

DRAWINGS:

*(a) HEH: 4 13/16 x 8 9/16 in.; watermark 1814; pen and watercolor with preparatory pencil; unfinished; verso: slight pencil sketch.

(b) Formerly with Frank T. Sabin: pen and watercolor; several minor variations from the print.

The theme of Death and the doctors is one Rowlandson employs frequently. Five of the published designs for the Dance of Death involve variations on the subject. A closely related drawing, but without the figure of Death, is in the collection of Dr. Morris Saffron.

69. DEATH AND THE ANTIQUARIES

PRINT:

Pub. Feby. 1, 1816, at R. Ackermann's, 101 Strand.

Death, jealous of his rights, stands sentry
Over this strange, burglarious entry.

4 15/16 x 8½ in.

All impressions in the Huntington Library appear to be of the same state. The normal color scheme has the man with an eyeglass, who is stooping forward, in purple; the man standing above and behind him, in green.

DRAWINGS:

*(a) HEH: 5 11/16 x 9 3/16 in.; pen and watercolor with preparatory pencil; numerous variations from the print, the most important being that the background is an open ruin. Inscribed verso (in what appears to be Rowlandson's hand):

I doe love these auncient vyynes
We never tread upon them but we set
Our foote upon some reverend History,
And questionless here in this open Court
Which now lies naked to the injuries
Of stormy weather, some men lye enterred
Loved the Church so well & gave so largely tot
They thought it should have canopied their
bones
Till Domesday, but all things have their end.
Churches & Cities (which have diseases like
to men)
Must have like Death that we have.

Also inscribed on verso in another hand (possibly Combe's): "This suppose in Westminster Abbey one of them stealing a ring and pulls of [sic] the finger at the same time."

(b) HEH: 5 x 8⅝ in.; pen and watercolor; unfinished; much closer to the print than (a); some numerals (apparently an account) on the verso.

It is possible that Rowlandson may be alluding to the celebrated opening of the coffin of Charles I in April 1813. The precise whereabouts of the coffin had been a mystery until it was accidentally discovered by some workmen during reconstruction work at St. George's Chapel, Windsor, in 1813. There was apparently some despoliation of the remains, and the royal physician, Henry Halford (who was present when the coffin was opened), obtained a portion of the fourth cervical vertebra, which had been cut by the headsman's axe.

70. THE DAINTY DISH

PRINT:

Pubd. March 1, 1816, at R. Ackermann's, 101 Strand.

This fine, hot, feast's a preparation
To some, for Death's last, cold, Collation.

4 13/16 x 7 13/16 in.

Second state: the back wall behind the clock has a two-tone wash of aquatint. The normal color scheme has the walls in pink, the man seated at the head of the table in blue.

DRAWING:

* HEH: 4⅞ x 7 15/16 in.; pen and watercolor with preparatory pencil; unfinished.

71. THE LAST STAGE

PRINT:

Pub. March 1, 1816, at R. Ackermann's, 101 Strand.

From Hour to Hour, from Youth to Age,
Life's Trav'ller takes th'uncertain Stage.

4¾ x 7 11/16 in.

The impressions in the Huntington Library all appear to be of the same state. The color schemes vary considerably, but the woman being helped into the coach is normally in yellow, the woman behind her in pink.

DRAWING:

* NYP: in reverse; 4¾ x 7 11/16 in.; pen and watercolor; the sign is inscribed "Here Inns the York / Edinburgh, Glasgow / Stage Coaches. / Mourning Coaches Lent." The drawing clearly began as a counterproof but has been reinforced throughout.

72. TIME, DEATH, AND ETERNITY

PRINT:

Pubd. March 1, 1816, at R. Ackermann's, 101 Strand.

The song now bursts beyond the bounds of time,
And Immortality concludes the Rhyme.
4 13/16 x 7 11/16 in.

Second state: aquatint is added to the ends of the masonry blocks immediately above Time's right wing. The normal color scheme has Time's robe in purple.

DRAWINGS:

*(a) HEH: 4⅞ x 7⅝ in.; pen over preparatory pencil (no wash).

(b) HEH: in reverse; 4⅞ x 7⅝ in.; pen and watercolor; clearly began as a counterproof pulled from (a).

Both these drawings are distinctly unusual in style, much more tightly drawn and finished than is normal for Rowlandson.

73. THE MAN OF FEELING

(unpublished)

DRAWINGS:

*(a) HEH: 4 15/16 x 8 3/16 in.; pen and watercolor with preparatory pencil; signed "Rowlandson"; mounted with the drawing is a handwritten label entitled "The Man of Feeling" followed by: "But in the Prison's transient gloom / May look for better times to come."

(b) HCL: 5½ x 8⅜ in.; pen and watercolor; signed and dated "Rowlandson 1820"; inscribed: "A friend in need is a friend indeed." The two drawings are probably related as tracings, although the sequence is not clear.

The subject, a release from prison and from Death, does not properly belong with a Dance of Death and may have been omitted for that reason. A variation on the subject, in which Death releases the debtor from prison, is No. 63 of the published designs.

74. THE OLD SUITOR REJECTED

(unpublished)

DRAWING:

* HEH: 5⅜ x 8½ in.; pen and watercolor with preparatory pencil.

Rowlandson used so many variations on the theme of youth and old age in marriage that it is not surprising to find yet another interpretation among the unpublished designs.

75. DEATH MIXING THE MORTAR

(unpublished)

DRAWING:

* HEH: 5¾ x 9⅜ in.; pen and watercolor with preparatory pencil.

76. DEATH AT THE DOOR

(unpublished)

DRAWING:

* HEH: 5⅝ x 9⅜ in.; pen and watercolor with preparatory pencil.

77. THE SWORD DUEL

(unpublished)

DRAWING:

* HEH: 5⅝ x 9⅜ in.; pen and watercolor with preparatory pencil. A spirited drawing which appears stylistically to be earlier than the majority of the Dance of Death series. The costumes imply either a masquerade or that Rowlandson wishes to suggest an earlier period. Rowlandson uses the duel theme once in the published designs (No. 35).

78. THE YOUNG FAMILY MOURNING IN THE CHURCHYARD

(unpublished)

DRAWINGS:

*(a) HEH: 5⅝ x 9 1/16 in.; pen and watercolor with preparatory pencil; one tombstone inscribed "Loving & / Tender / Husband / Aged 28"; another, "Sacred to the / Memory of."

(b) Philip Hofer: 5 15/16 x 9½ in.; pen and watercolor; a few differences from (a), notably the absence of the inscriptions.

The two drawings are probably related as tracings, but the sequence is not clear. Rowlandson does employ the theme of Death and the family more than once in the published designs. The figure of Death is very much less prominent here than in most of the designs for the series.

79. DEATH IN A BALLROOM

(unpublished)

DRAWING:

* HEH: 5¾ x 9 5/16 in.; pen and watercolor; unfinished; inscribed: "A Rude intruder rush'd into a private Ballroom and disturbed the whole Company."

This is exactly the theme of one of the published designs (No. 24) and might be a variant composition for that subject.

80. DEATH HELPING AN OLD LOVER INTO BED

(unpublished)

DRAWINGS:

*(a) HEH: 5 9/16 x 9 3/16 in.; pen and watercolor.

(b) HCL: 5 11/16 x 9⅛ in.; pen and watercolor.

The two drawings are probably connected by tracing, but the sequence is not clear.

81. RELEASED FROM DEATH

(unpublished)

DRAWINGS:

*(a) HEH: 5 11/16 x 9¼ in.; pen and watercolor with preliminary pencil; inscribed "Released from Death"; the lid of the coffin inscribed "Come to Life Again."

(b) HCL: 5 11/16 x 9⅛ in.; pen and watercolor.

One drawing is probably a tracing from the other, but the sequence is not clear.

82. DEATH AND THE BUTCHER

(unpublished)

DRAWING:

* HEH: 5 ¾ x 9 5/16 in.; pen and watercolor with preliminary pencil.

83. THE BARBER SHOP

(unpublished)

DRAWINGS:

*(a) HEH: 5¾ x 9 5/16 in.; pen and watercolor with preliminary pencil; verso inscribed (in Rowlandson's hand): "Smooth Chin Death a bad customer to the barber / The bold Barber or a sworn enemy to Death / A Struggle twixt life & Death."

(b) HEH: 5 11/16 x 9 5/16 in.; pen and watercolor with preliminary pencil; very close to (a) but more carefully elaborated; probably began as a tracing from (a). Lantern inscribed "Shaving / Bleeding / Tooth Draw."

(c) Formerly with Fitz Eugene Dixon of Philadelphia; present whereabouts unknown: 5¾ x 9⅜ in. American Art Association, January 6 and 7, 1937, Lot 139.

84. THE PUMP ROOM DOOR

(unpublished)

DRAWINGS:

*(a) HEH: 5 11/16 x 9¼ in.; pen and watercolor with preliminary pencil; the street sign on the corner of the building reads "South Parade"; above the door, "Pump Room"; to the left of the door, "Setts Off / every Hour / to Kingdom / come— / Road rather / Rough & / D . . ."; to right, "Places / taken / here / for Deaths / Dilly." There is some undecipherable writing on the verso.

(b) HEH: 5⅝ x 9¼ in.; pen and watercolor with preliminary pencil; the signs are inscribed as in (a) but with insignificant differences.

One drawing began as a tracing from the other, but the sequence is not clear. The scene is presumably outside the Pump Room at Bath.

85. DEATH AS POSTILION

(unpublished)

DRAWING:

* HEH: 5⅜ x 9 1/16 in.; pen and watercolor; the appearance of many of the lines suggests that a counterproof was pulled.

The general theme of death in a carriage accident is one that Rowlandson used frequently in the published designs. This particular subject is close to "The Fall of Four in Hand" (No. 42).

86. THE OLD LADY AFIRE

(unpublished)

DRAWINGS:

* Philip Hofer: 5 15/16 x 9½ in.; pen and watercolor.

87. DEATH IN THE DISSECTION ROOM

(unpublished)

DRAWING:

* NYP: 4 15/16 x 8 1/16 in.; pen and watercolor.

88. DEATH GARROTING A PRISONER

(unpublished)

DRAWING:

* NYP: 4 11/16 x 8 in.; pen and watercolor with preliminary pencil.

89. DEATH AND THE HIGHWAYMAN

(unpublished)

DRAWING:

*(a) NYP: 5⅝ x 9 5/16 in.; pen and watercolor with preliminary pencil. There is a pen drawing in

the Huntington Library that is closely related to the figure of the man.

(b) Formerly with Fitz Eugene Dixon of Philadelphia; present whereabouts unknown: 5 13/16 x 9½ in. Signed "T. Rowlandson." American Art Association, January 6 and 7, 1937, Lot 140.

90. DEATH AND THE DOCTOR LEAVING THE SICKROOM

(unpublished)

DRAWING:

* NYP: 4⅝ x 7 13/16 in.; pen and watercolor with preliminary pencil. The appearance of some of the lines suggests that a counterproof may have been pulled.

This theme is one that Rowlandson used frequently in the published designs.

91. DEATH ENTERING A SICKROOM THROUGH A WINDOW

(unpublished)

DRAWING:

* NYP: 5 7/16 x 8⅝ in.; pen and watercolor with preliminary pencil.

92. THE GAMESTER'S EXIT

(unpublished)

DRAWINGS:

*(a) HCL: 5⅛ x 7 in.; pen and watercolor; inscribed "A Gamester's Exit."

(b) NYP: 5 1/16 x 8 in.; pen and watercolor; signed (clipped) "Rowlandson."

(c) Ashmolean: 5 x 8¼ in.; pen and watercolor; signed "Rowlandson." On the old mount there is a handwritten label with the title "The Suicide" followed by:

Death smiles and seems his dart to hide
When he beholds the Suicide.

This is the same caption that appears on the print of "The Suicide" (No. 37 of the published series). Also on the old mount in pencil in a mid-nineteenth-century hand is the word "Copy." Drawings (b) and (c) are probably related as tracings, but the sequence is not clear. Said to be a copy by Miss Howitt (see Introduction, pp. 19-25).

93. DEATH PULLING A FAT MAN IN A WHEELCHAIR

(unpublished)

DRAWING:

* NYP: 4 1/16 x 7 in.; pen and watercolor; the drawing was inscribed but the inscription has been largely cut off.

94. NAILING THE COFFIN

(unpublished)

DRAWING:

* HCL: 5 11/16 x 9⅛ in.; pen and watercolor.

95. THE ASSASSINATION

(unpublished)

DRAWING:

* HCL: 5 9/16 x 9 3/16 in.; pen and watercolor.

96. DEATH REJOICING AT A NAVAL BATTLE

(unpublished)

DRAWING:

* HCL: 5⅛ x 8¼ in.; pen and watercolor; with collector's mark of Sir W. A. Fraser (Frits Lugt, *Les marques de collections de dessins & d'estampes*, No. 2830).

97. DEATH AND THE KNIGHT

(unpublished)

DRAWING:

* HCL: 5⅞ x 9⅜ in.; pen and watercolor.

98. DEATH AND THE DEBAUCHEE

(unpublished)

DRAWING:

* Paul Mellon: 5⅜ x 8½ in.; pen and watercolor; inscribed "Death and the Debauchéé" [sic].

99. THE PRISONER'S MEAL

(unpublished)

DRAWING:

* HCL: 5⅛ x 8⅛ in.; pen and watercolor.

100. DEATH AND THE NABOB

(unpublished)

DRAWING:

* The Art Museum, Princeton University: 5½ x 8¾ in.; pen and watercolor. The style and format of this drawing connect it with the *English Dance of Death* series, although the subject is obviously not English.